THIS IS THE DAY—

Encouraging words to accompany your day

Part One : January-June

THIS IS THE DAY–
Encouraging words to accompany your Day
Part One: January-June

ISBN: 978-0-9955524-9-4

All Rights Reserved. Copyright © 2019 Thank You Jesus Books

No part of this book may be reproduced or transmitted in any form or by any means, graphic, electronic, or mechanical, including photocopying, recording, taping or by any information storage or retrieval system, without the permission in writing from the copyright holder.

Published by Thank You Jesus Books
Divine Favour Enterprises Ltd
P.O. Box 10649
Loughborough,
LE11 9JQ
UK

www: peprah-gyamfi.com
Email: info@peprah-gyamfi.com

All Scripture references, unless otherwise indicated, are from the King James Version

THIS IS THE DAY–
Encouraging words to accompany your day
Part One : January-June

R. Peprah-Gyamfi

THANK YOU JESUS BOOK LTD

This *is* the day the Lord has made; we will rejoice and be glad in it.

— Psalm 118:24

Foreword

The Christian posts in this volume have given me great encouragement in my daily walk of faith and I am not at all surprised that in Facebook they have generated a staggering number of over 140 000 followers in less than three months! Without doubt I can commend them to you, dear reader, now collected in this handy book which you can keep by your bedside or take with you wherever you go. It will ensure that your spiritual battery is constantly charged; in times of discouragement or fear it will remind you of the unlimited grace, love, protection and power of our Lord Jesus.

You will find that each post has a coherent structure, beginning with a biblical text that is then elucidated from the author's own life experience—often from his impoverished childhood in Ghana, or from his experience and knowledge as a medical doctor. The biblical texts are chosen with care, invariably with a view to reassure you that God is close and cares for you, ever ready to rescue you from danger, from fear, from despair, from depression, to turn around your life when you draw close to him. As I said, the messages are vividly illustrated from the Bible. One of my favourite messages is that we have a 'turn-around' God—illustrated by the life of Joseph whose life was turned around from captive and slave to Prime Minister! The message or theme that I like best is that God makes all things new! Through his miraculous power, Jesus, our divine doctor, cures ailments not by healing but by re-creating. God is our creator, so in effect Jesus 'heals' by accessing and releasing the original principle and power of creation—as in the case of the resurrected Lazarus; he *creates*, whether it be a new body or a new organ, that *replaces* the diseased or injured organ. The author is a medical doctor himself, remember, so he is well qualified as a born-again Christian doctor, to recognise such medical mysteries. Through his guidance in these posts you are putting your mind in touch with the 'turn-around' God who has the means to *re-create* you—your mind and your body. Just think of that!

It has been a privilege that I have known the author, Dr Robert Peprah-Gyamfi, for over fourteen years now. Our friendship began in 2004 when I became his editor and portal to publishing his first book *The Call that Changed my Life*. This is a remarkable Christian autobiography that reveals his great courage and faith in making his strenuous and challenging journey from Ghana, via a Nigerian building site, to Germany where, in spite of all odds, he learnt the German language and qualified as a medical doctor at a prestigious German university. But he had heeded the call to become a servant of the living Jesus in a vision he received way back in Ghana and so he knew his dream of becoming a doctor in Geramy was vouchsafed. I recommend this book to you, reader, as an encouraging testimony of faith and belief in our 'turn-around' God. The author has published many books but my favourite is *Doctor Jesus: The Doctor Who Knows No Bounds*—in which the author stresses that the Healing Ministry of Doctor Jesus did not end with His death, resurrection and ascension and that even to this day those who genuinely invoke His Name in childlike faith can expect astonishing miracles, including the healing of diseases that have baffled conventional medical practice. It is more than a healing ministry of course, as the posts in this new book reveal—because the essence of divine healing is more than healing, it is re-creating by the God of creation who makes all things new!

I commend these books to you, dear reader—and indeed all of the works by Dr Peprah-Gyamfi—and now, especially, the collection of posts in this new book that speak directly to the heart and mind of the Christian soldier on the battlefield of life.

Charles H. Muller,
MA (Wales), PhD (London), DEd (SA), DLitt (UF)

January 1

****
Remember ye not the former things, neither consider the things of old. Behold, I will do a new thing; now it shall spring forth; shall ye not know it? I will even make a way in the wilderness, and rivers in the desert.

– Isaiah 43:18-19
****

A new year has been ushered in; the past year has become history. Whereas you and I have no idea of what lies ahead of us, I AM THAT I AM does!

Yes indeed, from the very moment that you are reading this piece, right through to December 31 and beyond, everything, and by that I really mean everything, is known to Him.

Not only does He know in advance what will happen to the universe, He also has foreknowledge of what lies ahead for each and every individual populating the surface of the earth up to the very last second of midnight December 31, 2019—and beyond!

I have drawn attention to the above for a purpose—to remind fellow Christian soldiers that we have a Friend, yes, a Commander-in-Chief who knows the end from the beginning, so we need not be afraid, come what may!

I want at this stage to invite my fellow Christian warrior to join me in casting any fears we are entertaining for the just begun year—and indeed beyond—into the dustbin. Our battle cry should indeed be "No fears yesterday, no fears today, no fears for tomorrow and beyond!"

We should indeed draw inspiration from today's verse and face the future with full confidence.

Even more important, I pray the Lord of Heaven and Earth to grant us the grace and favour required for an even closer walk with Him.

Finally, on the basis of today's scriptures, I am taking authority in the Mighty Name of the Lord to declare a breakthrough on all fronts for myself and my fellow Christian soldiers. A breakthrough at home and outside of the home; a breakthrough in health and finance—breakthrough through here, breakthrough there, breakthrough through everywhere!

There is indeed a future of hope for us and surely our hope will not be cut off!

(Proverbs 23:18)

Happy New Year to myself and everyone!

January 2

****
In the sweat of thy face shalt thou eat bread, till thou return unto the ground; for out of it wast thou taken: for dust thou art, and unto dust shalt thou return.

– Genesis 3:19
****

Human beings have over the years invested much effort and resources to tackle diseases of all kind. Just as you are reading through these lines, somewhere in the world, in the sophisticated laboratories of chemical and pharmaceutical giants such as AstraZeneca, Bayer, Eli Lilly, Pfizer, etc., advanced experiments are under way to discover the cure for hitherto incurable diseases such as HIV, various kinds of motor neurone diseases, various forms of cancer and also to improve the qualities of some of the drugs already in use in the fight against various forms of diseases.

In one aspect of our existence, namely in the matter of death, however, try as the most sophisticated brains among us would, we remain powerless. As it was yesterday, so it is today, and so it will continue to be, for so it has been ordained by The Giver of life, the Master of Creation, the 'I am that I am', Jehovah Jireh, God the Almighty, God the Omnipotent and Omnipresent.

As Christian soldiers, we need not fear the inevitable fate of mortal man, though, for indeed our Commander-in-Chief has boldly declared:

"I am the resurrection and the life. He who believes in Me, though he may die, he shall live. And whoever lives and believes in Me shall never die. Do you believe this?"

John 6:25-26 (KJV)

January 3

****

He answered and said, Whether he be a sinner or no, I know not: one thing I know, that, whereas I was blind, now I see.

– **John 9:25**

****

For the sake of those not familiar with the story, I shall provide a short background:

> Jesus was passing with His disciples. They saw a man born blind. Jesus mixed his saliva with some mud and applied the mixture to his eyes and urged him to go and wash in the Pool of Siloam.

He was healed in the process and went about glorifying God. Eventually he was brought before the Pharisees. They accused Jesus of breaking the Sabbath and urged the healed to give glory to God, but not Jesus whom they regard as a sinner. It was in the course of the discourse that the person who had benefitted from the miraculous healing encounter made the compelling statement: *Whether he be a sinner or no, I know not: one thing I know, that, whereas I was blind, now I see.*

Oh, what a statement! I beg to make it my own—

"Whether he be a sinner or no, I know not: one thing I know, that, whereas I was blind, now I see." Hallelujah! Praise the Lord! Thank you, Jesus, thank you Lord, thank you for healing a blind man like me; glory, glory to You! I earnestly wish the blind man was around today! I would extend an invitation to him and urge him to repeat that statement several times in my hearing, if he would. Lost in sin and blind to spiritual things, the Lord called me and gave me hope not only in regard to this world, but also the hope of everlasting life.

Of course, you and I know, Christian warriors, that our Commander in Chief is sinless; indeed, we even know that He is the Son of God who sets the sinner free.

Yes, we care less about those who say and publish all sorts of things to discredit our Saviour. Indeed, no matter what the unbeliever might do or say to discredit our Lord, you and I can declare with all boldness and confidence, notwithstanding allegations that He may be "this and/or that", that we *know* above all – that whereas we were blinded by sin, now we see!

January 4

****

He will not suffer thy foot to be moved: he that keepeth thee will not slumber. Behold, he that keepeth Israel shall neither slumber nor sleep.

– **Psalm 121:3-4**

****

When faced with drawbacks and hurdles in our Christian walk, and our prayers seem to fall on deaf ears, we seem to think that perhaps God is overstrained, so occupied responding to the prayers of His children elsewhere on the globe, that He may not have ears for our own problems. By our attitudes we seem to create the impression that we cannot imagine how the same person could simultaneously respond to:

> The prayers of a resident in New Zealand imploring Him to protect him/ her as he/she retires to bed at the end of the day;
>
> A mighty man of God calling on Him to cast out demons and heal the sick at a big revival meeting taking place in the afternoon of the same day in Nairobi;

The little girl in Los Angeles imploring Him to guide and guard her through the same day that is about to begin there.

'Maybe Our God is resting for a while! We better allow Him time to enjoy His deserved respite and not disturb Him.' So we decide to seek help elsewhere – Astrology, New Age thinking, Juju, Voodoo! We consult the soothsayers, to plead with them to reveal the future to us, to tell us what lies in store for us in the future! Thus going around to let others reveal the future to us! Who controls the future in the first place!? So we read our stars everyday to know what the stars have in store for us! The stars – what are the stars when you are resting in a God who never changes – and who made the stars?!

Why do we want to know what the stars have in store for us when the Good Lord of heaven and earth, has sent the Holy Spirit to dwell in us? Are we not aware of the Divine assurance that "greater is He that is in you than He that is in the world?" (I John 4:4)

We do not indeed need to know what the stars have in store for us, for we are assured in Psalm 23:6 that goodness and mercy shall follow us all the days of our life!

Yes for sure "he that keepeth Israel shall neither slumber nor sleep", so let's remain calm and collected and not waver in the face of the challenges of life.

January 5

****

Trust in the LORD with all thine heart; and lean not unto thine own understanding. In all thy ways acknowledge him, and he shall direct thy paths.

– Proverbs 3:5-6

****

Indeed, if we have the God of Jacob as our friend, if indeed we have left all to follow the Good Shepherd, then we have to learn to trust Him to direct our steps for good.

Apparent disappointments may come our way, but we are assured in Romans 8:28 (KJV) that "all things work together for good to them that love God, to them who are the called according to his purpose."

For sure, all things will work together for us, probably not in the way we had anticipated, but He who knows the end form the beginning knows what is best for us. Aware that the journey we are about to embark upon will end in catastrophe, it is in His nature to preserve us, His loving ones from danger. Our tyre may burst even before we set off; electric malfunctions may prevent the engine from starting; our gears may fail to engage. We who can only see the present are inclined under such circumstances to react angrily!

If only He would open our eyes to reveal to us the dangers ahead of us, we would cease from murmuring. Dear Christian friends, if we have put our trust in the Lord, let us learn to accept whatever comes our way, however unpalatable.

January 6

****
What shall we say then? Shall we continue in sin, that grace may abound? God forbid. How shall we, that are dead to sin, live any longer therein?

– Romans 6:1-2
****

As a student in Germany I earned extra income by working as a translator in my mother tongue, the Twi language (spoken in Ghana) for the authorities, including the police.

On one occasion the law enforcing agents needed me to translate the telephone conversations – both recorded and live – of an individual suspected of belonging to an international drug smuggling ring.

As it turned out the suspect had a girlfriend who was engaged in prostitution in the red-light area of the city. On one occasion the lady called her friend to complain bitterly about the worsening business climate, indeed about the fall in the number of clients she was receiving. In her exasperation she cried out: "Please Lord Jesus, help me today by drawing a decent number of clients to my booth!" I prayed the Lord to save her from her crooked ways, for she was, in effect, bending the rules to suit her own end.

"Shall we continue in sin, that grace may abound? God forbid. How shall we, that are dead to sin, live any longer therein?"

Dear Christian friend, let's pray the good Lord for the grace required to walk in the path of righteousness, today and for ever more. May His Name be praised and glorified.

January 7

****

Now faith is the substance of things hoped for, the evidence of things not seen.

– Hebrews 11:1

****

Have faith in the Lord, child of God; have faith in the Lord –
faith that will enable you to stand and not fall,
even should the earth beneath you quake violently
and cause the strongest of mountains to shake to their very foundations.

Have faith in the Living Lord;
faith that is capable of penetrating the darkest of dark clouds
to provide the light to lead you home—
faith that will enable you to swim above
the deep clouds gathering around you.

Have faith in the King of Kings; faith that will enable you to discern the still peaceful voice of the Good Shepherd in the midst of the confusing noises buffeting you from all sides;
faith that will enable you to proclaim God's word without fear or favour.
Have faith in the Ancient of Days, child of God;
faith that will enable you to swim against the tide of time;
faith that will enable you to stand and be counted in the defence of Divine truth in an increasingly godless world.

JANUARY 8

****
Whosoever cometh to me, and heareth my sayings, and doeth them, I will shew you to whom he is like: He is like a man which built a house, and digged deep, and laid the foundation on a rock: and when the flood arose, the stream beat vehemently upon that house, and could not shake it: for it was founded upon a rock.

– Luke 6:47-48
****

We live in a globalised world. From time to time television, the internet as well as other media outlets, bring raging storms, hurricanes, typhoons, etc., right into our living rooms. Though not physically present, we are enabled to have a glimpse of the force behind the ferocious hurricanes and typhoons and the catastrophic high winds and deadly storm surges associated with them.

The Lord is saying that whoever listens to His words and does them is like a person who has built his house on a rock – the type of house capable of withstanding tornadoes, hurricanes and typhoons however ferocious.

Such types of buildings are not spared the battering by the monstrous storms. The tempests and cyclones and what-have-you may indeed succeed in ripping off their roofs and shattering their window; yet try as the elements may, they can never succeed in uprooting them! Why should they when they are grounded on the Rock, yes, the Power that holds the whole Universe in His hands!

JANUARY 9

But he that heareth, and doeth not, is like a man that without a foundation built a house upon the earth; against which the stream did beat vehemently, and immediately it fell; and the ruin of that house was great.

– Luke 6:49

The Lord compares those who are grounded in Him, yes those who have built their houses on a rock, to those who are not with Him, yes those who have built their houses on sand. Some call themselves atheists, some refer to themselves as agnostics, still others describe themselves as humanists, etc. They either reject entirely the existence of God, or they think He is irrelevant in human affairs

Then there are the acclaimed stars, celebrities, public figures. They may not reject the existence of God, but have no time for Him and His word. They enjoy the limelight, the fame, the wealth, the human acclaim, etc.

They have built on sand. Let the storms of life set in – diseases that prevent them from performing, a crash on the stock exchange that causes their wealth to be wiped away in the twinkle of the eye, a break in relationships that shatters their hopes and they fall and crash so low some find in suicide the only avenue of escape! Not grounded on the rock, but rather built on sand, such individuals are easily swept away by the hurricanes and typhoons of life.

It is our duty, fellow soldiers of the Cross, to do all we can to bring the message of salvation and the hope to the world, yes to direct the world to the Rock of Ages, so they may securely build on Him, instead of on the loose, shifting sands of life.

JANUARY 10

> **And Elisha prayed, and said, LORD, I pray thee, open his eyes, that he may see. And the LORD opened the eyes of the young man; and he saw: and, behold, the mountain was full of horses and chariots of fire round about Elisha.**
>
> **– 2 Kings 6:17**

Open his eyes, that he may see!

Elisha's servant was not physically blind. No, he was not, he could see clearly. Physically he could see quite clearly; indeed, he was able to behold the invading army from a distance; and yet he was afflicted with a different kind of blindness – spiritual blindness.

I personally have made it a habit not to argue with those who claim to be atheists. Rather than argue with them, I pray for them. I am reminded in this connection of Apostle Paul in his days as Saul of Tarsus – yes, at the time when he was persecuting the church; do you think at that time he would have listened to anyone who came to him to argue his case about the reality of the Crucified Christ? I am not saying we should not make efforts to tell them about our faith. We should however desist from argument, prolonged arguments.

The blind Saul, the persecutor of the church, needed to have his eyes opened to see beyond the here and now and into the spiritual reality.

The atheist indeed has a physical perspective. What he or she needs is spiritual insight, and that cannot be attained, by our efforts, but through grace. So it is imperative for us, fellow Christian soldiers, to pray for such individuals, that a higher power might be invoked to sweep away their blindness.

January 11

****

When the unclean spirit is gone out of a man, he walketh through dry places, seeking rest; and finding none, he saith, I will return unto my house whence I came out. And when he cometh, he findeth it swept and garnished. Then goeth he, and taketh to him seven other spirits more wicked than himself; and they enter in, and dwell there: and the last state of that man is worse than the first

– Luke 11:24-26

****

There is a saying that 'nature abhors a vacuum'. The saying expresses the fact that empty or unfilled spaces are unnatural as they go against the laws of nature and physics. Nature abhors a vacuum. What is true in the physical world is also true in the spiritual. There can be no spiritual vacuum in the life of an individual whether they like it or not. No one can indeed exist in a vacuum in the midst of the spiritual battle raging today. For sure, no one can assume neutrality.

The atheist, yes, he or she who does not believe in God, may want to assume neutrality in the matter. If only he or she would come to the realisation that that is not possible.

Almighty God does indeed give us the choice to decide. He does not force anyone to take sides. It is not His nature to force our coerce humanity, the product of His own creation, into worshiping Him.

Whereas Almighty God accepts spiritual neutrality, indeed does not force His will on anyone, the Devil is not so forthcoming. In fact, Satan, a.k.a. Lucifer and the demons who do to his bidding, do not recognize neutrality. They go around looking for hearts devoid of Light from above – the Light they are unable to withstand. The moment they identify any such vacancy, they force themselves in, uninvited, and entrench themselves there. Yes, certainly, Satan will occupy the void in an individual whether he or she likes it or not.

Dear Christian soldier, if indeed we have accepted the Lord into our lives, let's hold tenaciously to our hope and not allow anything to distract us from our goal.

January 12

The Lord is my light and Salvation; whom shall I fear? The Lord is the strength of my life; of whom shall I be afraid?

– Psalm 27:1

Do not murmur the words; do not declare them with a low voice. No, say it loud! Shout, scream, yell! Declare it at the top of your voice. Indeed, that is the attitude we have to adopt towards the great deceiver. For, certainly, Satan does not understand diplomatic language. No, diplomatic language should be left to the diplomats who are trained to choose their words with the aim of promoting cordial international relationships. Why the need for us to practice the art of word-weighing when we are confronted by a foe bent on destroying us at all cost?

How often do we hear people these days say things like – I am scared; it is frightening! I am scared; I am nervous, I am apprehensive! Even we, the sons and daughters of the Rock of Ages, yes, the children of the Good Shepherd, souls He has purchased with His own blood, are often heard telling the whole world how much we are afraid, or scared or apprehensive of this and that!

Not so David in this psalm; yes, he is declaring that come what may, he does not care, he does not bother – he does not mind! He is telling Satan to his face: "Hey you, don't dare venture near my place of abode, near my husband, near my wife, near my children, near my place of work, near my car whether it is parked or in motion, near my business, near my bank accounts!" In short, he is telling Lucifer and all the demons under his control to his face that they can just go and get drowned in the mighty ocean!

Let us face this day, my dear Christian friend assured that our Lord is with us, so we need not fear – come what may!

JANUARY 13

****
> **Why art thou cast down, O my soul? and why art thou disquieted in me? hope thou in God: for I shall yet praise him for the help of his countenance.**
>
> – Psalm 42:5

****

Are you undergoing struggles, trials, disappointments?

You are looking for a job. You have left no stone unturned.

You have invested your energy, time and resources to put your application together only to receive one rejection letter after the other.

At long last, a call for an interview! You put your best foot forward; yes, you invest time, energy to prepare for the upcoming interview.

You are optimistic you will get the job this time round!

You leave home several hours ahead of schedule, to ensure you get the job.

The interview goes well – at least that is the impression you get as you make your homeward journey. 'I am going to get the job, I am surely going to get the job!'

You wait several days; contrary to the promise given to you, no one calls. You pick up the phone, call to find out what is happening—

"Sorry, but you were not successful."

Throughout the day, you are downcast. 'Why, me, why me?'

Hold on, my dear Christian friend!

Well, I too went through the same experience several times!

Don't give up your faith friend, don't give up. Stand firm.

The saying indeed is true – when God closes a door, He opens a window! You can be sure of that! Yes, you can bet on it.

The waiting may prove wearisome though, but stand, stand firm.

Based on my own experience, I can assure you, fellow Christians, that our God, whom we serve, will surely make a way when there seems to be no way.

So get up, dear Christian soldier, and keep jumping for Jesus – for we are indeed overcomers!

JANUARY 14

***

God is our refuge and strength, a very present help in trouble.

– Psalm 46:1

***

During the time I worked as a doctor in various hospitals in Germany, I did emergency duty with the ambulance service from time to time. The emergency doctor accompanied by one or two paramedics was dispatched in an ambulance to provide assistance for patients with life-threatening conditions.

Even as I write, I have a vivid memory of one particular case that required our rapid intervention. It involved a patient who developed an anaphylactic reaction, yes a life-threatening condition in reaction to a bee sting. The lady in question was relaxing in her garden around midday on a beautiful day in summer when she was stung by a bee. The severe allergic reaction set in moments later. Soon she could hardly breathe! Fortunately, she was not alone at home. The astonished relatives alerted the emergency services without delay.

We managed to reach her quickly enough to prevent the worst from happening – indeed she made a complete recovery.

Circumstances beyond our control could have delayed our arrival though. Indeed, in some instances, we had, despite the priority we had on the road, no choice but to stop to give other forms of traffic the right of way – for instance, when we came to a railway crossing that had its barriers lowered.

God is a present help in time of trouble, declares the Psalmist. Indeed, as far as he is concerned, even before the bee stings to discharge its venom or toxin to threaten the life of His child known to have bee sting allergy, God is already present providing first aid!

Boasting such an able Commander-in-Chief, let us, fellow Christian soldier, with all boldness perform our duties on the battlefield of life and not become weary of the forces bent on annihilating us!

JANUARY 15

****

But thou, O Daniel, shut up the words, and seal the book, even to the time of the end: many shall run to and fro, and knowledge shall be increased.

– Daniel 12:4

****

We live in a fast-changing world. Not only has knowledge increased; the revolution in information technology has led to a situation whereby we are today bombarded with a flood of information – truths, half-truths, fake news.

Not only are we exposed to an ever-changing flood of information, the opinions and attitudes of society to various issues keep on changing all the time. What was shunned by society yesterday becomes the norm today, only to be discarded tomorrow.

Therein lies the conflict Humanity versus God! We serve a God who CHANGETH NOT! Indeed, our God is the same yesterday, today and forever. The sons and daughters of men can change their minds here and there – that's their problem, not God's! The problem begins, though, when we, yes we mere products of flesh, seem to have the audacity to urge God to change His mind to, as it were, "move with the tide of time"!

My dear Christian friend, let us hold fast to Godly principles and resist the urge to swim with the crowd, indeed with the masses.

January 16

****

Shadrach, Meshach, and Abednego, answered and said to the king, O Nebuchadnezzar, we are not careful to answer thee in this matter. If it be so, our God whom we serve is able to deliver us from the burning fiery furnace, and he will deliver us out of thine hand, O king. But if not, be it known unto thee, O king, that we will not serve thy gods, nor worship the golden image which thou hast set up.

– Daniel 3:16-18

****

That is an extraordinary example of trust and faith in God. Facing the prospect of terrible death through burning in the oven, the three gallant soldiers of the Cross remained faithful to their calling! Thankfully, hardly any one of us alive today may be placed in a situation where we have to make a choice between holding on to our faith our being burnt in the oven.

What we face now is a spiritual warfare, yes, the battle against the spiritual powers of darkness, even demonic agents – Juju, Voodoo, witchcraft, etc. We should however not be intimidated by them. Let us indeed, like Shadrach, Meshach and Abednego, declare to the spiritual powers of darkness up against us that they may as well dispatch an e-mail to Nebuchadnezzar to urge him to heat his oven a thousand times above what he normally would to burn his enemies, for even so we are not afraid, nor scared, nor frightened of his threats!

Let us with one voice boldly declare:

"O Evil Tormentor of God's children, we do not need to defend ourselves before you in this matter. In regard to your incessant attacks on the children of God, we strongly believe that the God we serve is able to deliver us from your hand, O merciless Tormentor.

"But even if He does not, we want you to know, O you Evil one, that we will never be intimidated by your assaults nor allow ourselves to be cajoled by your insinuations to deny the Lord our Righteousness. Yes, come what may, we want to declare to the whole world that we shall NOT BOW DOWN TO YOU!"

January 17

****

It is better to take refuge in the Lord than to trust in humans. It is better to take refuge in the Lord than to trust in princes.

– Psalm 118:8-9

****

It is indeed important that we stand up to principle and not swim with the tide, or "Go with the Flow". Yes, when it comes to Christian principles, it is important we hold on to established principles. You may ask me which? My answer is to check the Bible; if in doubt I suggest you keep initially to the four Gospels. Later as you become more established in the faith, you can venture into "more difficult terrain". You may not understand everything, but I pray the Holy Spirit will lead and enlighten you to provide needed wisdom and strength.

There is indeed the tendency these days to "Go with the Flow." "Everyone on social media finds it okay so it must be right," I hear someone say. "BBC and CNN have given a positive review of a current specific trend in human relations, so it must be 'cool' to join the movement."

During my days as a medical student, I used to work as a carer in my free time to supplement my income. Though several years have now elapsed, I still have vividly in mind a middle-aged patient we supported at his home. He was an HIV patient in an advanced stage of the disease. Apart from providing basic care we did his shopping for him and occasionally wheeled him around the neighbourhood.

He was downhearted much of the time. He was never tired of expressing his disgust at his many male partners who had deserted him in his time of need. He was not blaming them for his situation, nor was he expecting them to be able to change the course of events.

He yearned however for at least occasional visits from them. In his time of need his former pals had deserted him.

We must indeed be careful how we go about our lives. When the world provides cheerleaders for a behaviour pattern, we soldiers of the Cross need to turn to the Word of God for the final say in the matter.

I pray the Lord bestows upon us the needed wisdom to make the right choices – decisions consistent with our Holy calling.

JANUARY 18

****

What is more, I consider everything a loss because of the surpassing worth of knowing Christ Jesus my Lord, for whose sake I have lost all things. I consider them garbage, that I may gain Christ.

– Philippians 3:8

****

I call myself medical doctor, author and servant of the Living Jesus. It is no boasting , because it reflects the facts.

In August 1984, I picked up me studies at the Hanover Medical School in Germany. After cracking and cracking my brains—yes after sacrificing, self-sacrificing associations, I finally qualified as doctor.

I have the passion for writing. Indeed I have been writing since my teenage years. I have in the meantime written 17 books—on Christianity, health education, stories centred around life in my village of birth etc.

On September 14, 1978, the Lord sent His servant to testify to His goodness. I followed her to church and committed myself to the Lord. Though not the perfect of servants, I do now refer to myself as a servant of the Living Jesus

"Will you want to sum up briefly your experience in the three "callings" you have just referred to?" I hear someone say.

Okay , here with go–

Concerning my title "doctor" experience, on not a few occasions, I have wished that I could rid myself of that designation. Indeed the title I acquired by virtue of a great deal of sacrifice and brain cracking , has become a burden , if not a curse. It has , among other things led others to associate me with wealth, yes considerable wealth—which I don't have! Others do not only hesitate to ask me for this and that favour, I have on a few occasions been the victim of fraud—by those who probably took me for rich by virtue of my designation.

My "Doctor" title has also not helped me as an author. Indeed, after I have spent hours on end writing and thereafter investing my own money to self-publish my work, some thinking I am a rich doctor seeking even more wealth have been reluctant to support me.

My own life experience has thought me the following: whilst there is nothing wrong for us to strive for high laurels , yes to acquire titles and honours, such titles and honours may end up being burdens and curses. If indeed, there is any honour, title , worthy of striving for, it is indeed that of Disciple/ Servant/ Soldier/ of the Living Jesus. It is indeed that title alone, that at the end of the day stands the test of time.

JANUARY 19

****
When my father and my mother forsake me, then the LORD will take me up.

– Psalm 27:10
****

When I arrived in Berlin several years ago (Berlin at the time was divided into West and East Berlin) a story made headlines in the Western part of the city.

It involved a lady whose dog needed surgery to cure a life-threatening condition. Since the individual involved did not have the means to pay for the treatment, she went to the press to launch an appeal for help. In her passionate appeal for assistance, the lady revealed to the whole world that her only living companion was the dog and that she could not imagine living without it: "If my dog dies, I will die!" Such was the bold headline in the tabloid that carried the news!

A very pitiful situation indeed! Much as I pitied the individual concerned, it gave me food for thought. How come an individual could develop such a deep bound with an animate being , yes to make the dog , her rock as it were.

Dear Christian soldier, do you feel deserted by the whole world? Do you feel lonely, lonely at home? Much as your children will like to keep you company, the stress of modern life, yes the fact that they also have to fend for themselves is making it difficult for them to visit regularly.

My heart goes with your lonely Christian soldier. You have not been deserted though. He who cares for the sparrows of the air and the lilies of the field will continue to keep you company, yes provide for you so cheer up, precious child of God.

January 20

****

For he shall give his angels charge over thee, to keep thee in all thy ways.

– Psalm 91:11

****

At the moment, it is generally regarded that the world we live in has only one remaining superpower. The president, the commander-in-chief, has the last say in the defence of that nation. So whenever danger strikes late at night and there needs to be a response, he has to be awakened from sleep.

You and I, let us ponder over it! Let us reflect over the matter for a moment. The commander-in-chief of the most powerful nation on earth, he who has the last say over the huge military arsenal at the disposal of that country, cannot withstand sleep and needs to be awakened!

That is not the calibre of the Commander-in-Chief under whose command Christian warriors are operating on the battlefield of life! No, the Ancient of Days, who spoke " let there be light and there was light" does not need to be awakened from sleep by the Chief of the Defence Staff of his Armed Forces to be briefed on the impending danger!!

When I was growing up in Ghana, my father possessed a small battery powered transistor radio. The brand name of one type of battery we fed to our radio is still vivid in my memory—Eveready Batteries.

Yes, Almighty God, has assigned his protecting angels to take charge of us His children, to offer eveready protection, yes to deliver, to rescue, to preserve us from evil.

So dear soldiers of the Cross, let us not shiver, nor panic, nor be frightened, no matter the dangers we are exposed to.

January 21

****

For I the LORD **thy God will hold thy right hand, saying unto thee, Fear not; I will help thee.**

– Isaiah 41:13

****

When I was growing up there was no school in our little village so we had to walk a distance of about three kilometres to attend the primary school at a comparatively larger village. When I got to Primary 5, something happened to me that threatened to bring about an abrupt end to my education. All of a sudden, and for no apparent cause, my left ankle began to swell up. Initially the accompanying discomfort was bearable, permitting me to continue to attend school. In time, however, the pain increased in intensity. Despite the increasing discomfort, I refused initially to stay out of school. I enjoyed going to school and stayed away only when it was absolutely impossible for me to go.

A time eventually came when no choice was left for me other than to stay at home. So unbearable was the pain that I could hardly stand on the affected leg. That interruption in my education lasted for two long years.

Just when the whole world seemed to have given up on me, the Lord of heaven and earth lifted up His hands and turned things around, not only to enable me to walk without a walking aid but also to enable me to resume my education.

Just in the same way the Lord turned things around for me, I trust him to turn around the situation of His children reading through these lines who are saddled with diverse problems.

Has your business collapsed? Have you out of disease, probably chronic low back pain been forced to give up your job? Have you lost your job and threatened with the repossession of your home as a result? Is everything falling apart around you? Has everyone given up on you—including yourself?

Well, hope in the Lord my friend; he is the friend of the friendless, hope for the despairing, good health for the terminally ill.

So keep on trusting the turn around God. He will surely visit your home, ere it is too late!

JANUARY 22

And when he thus had spoken, he cried with a loud voice, Lazarus, come forth. And he that was dead came forth, bound hand and foot with graveclothes: and his face was bound about with a napkin. Jesus saith unto them, Loose him, and let him go.

– John 11:43-44

At the grave of Lazarus, the Lord of Creation demonstrated, before several witnesses, His creation powers as infallible evidence for the doubters, sceptics, agnostics and what have you.

The Lord decided not even to touch the body of the dead to affect a direct transfer of His Creative powers. He chose instead just to send out the Word. Let us just ponder the matter! The mere sound waves that emanated from Him at the opening of His mouth carried enough Creation power to restore, in the time it takes to blink an eye, life back to the decomposing body of Lazarus.

At death all the trillion plus cells in our body suffer irreversible damage and cease to function. That is what science has found out to be the case; that is the scientific reality. Well, you can throw scientific reality to the dogs in the presence of the Supernatural One! Throw them into the garbage bin, my friend. Indeed, at the command 'Lazarus, come forth!' all the trillion plus cells in the body of the dead man, cells that had suffered irreversible damage, became instantaneously active and functional. They did not undergo repair, mind you! No they were re-created by He who created everything to begin with!.

Dear Christian soldier! Please do not allow the so-called learned of our day, who are going about spreading the falsehood of evolution and all the lies associated with it confuse or deceive you. We are indeed wonderfully created by Almighty God!

Stay blessed, my dear fellow soldier of the Cross of Calvary.

JANUARY 23

****
Great is our Lord, and of great power: his understanding is infinite.

– Psalm 147:5
****

The problem with humanity is that we tend to place limitations on the power and authority of Almighty God. Limited as the brain is in scope of understanding –it is even not able to understand itself!—we tend to think that applies in the case of Almighty God as well.

When the Bible, for example, teaches that Almighty God caused the Red Sea to part in two to allow Moses and the Israelites to walk on dry land, the atheist, the Darwinists, the sceptics and what have you, respond with statements like: that is a fairy tale, a fairy tale that only the unenlightened can believe! Such a deed is physically impossible; no never can that be!

Impossible, too hard, too difficult! Impossible—for whom? Hard—for whom? Difficult—for whom? Imagine setting artificial boundaries on Divine Authority! Placing natural barriers on what the Lord can do and cannot do! Placing scientific limitations on the ability of the Divine to intervene in the affairs of His world!

We may have our doubts as to whether Almighty God is capable of causing the Red Sea to part to allow His will to be fulfilled. That is our problem—not His! He might as well cause the Atlantic Ocean to part to allow His chosen ones to drive on dry land from Scotland to Canada or the East Coast of the USA! Placing restrictions on the power and might of the Lord of Host—imagine!

My fellow Christian soldiers, let us pray the Lord, to increase our faith, faith that will give us victory over our doubts and reservations.

JANUARY 24

****

But Simon's wife's mother lay sick of fever, and anon they tell him of her. And he came and took her by the hand, and lifted her up; and immediately the fever left her, and she ministered unto them.

– Mark 1:30-31

****

The Lord of Creation came to the home of Peter's mother-in-law, was confronted with the sad manifestation of disease and conquered it. He did not do so in ordinary fashion. He did not, for example, in the spirit of political correctness, appeal to the disease to leave the body of the afflicted at its own choosing, in a gentle, gradual manner. Instead, the Bible records that the fever departed instantly; *sofort*, as the Germans might put it!

That the disease should take flight immediately and vanish in the presence of Almighty God, does not surprise me, personally. What else is to be expected when the Lord of Creation, the Power above powers, the Authority above all authority, the Commander-in-Chief above all commanders-in-chief confronts disease head on? It should indeed be a foregone conclusion. Unfortunately this is not appreciated, for sadly we live in a world that, increasingly, has become atheistic—yes, one that denies the existence of the Almighty God. which amounts to denying the existence of the Supernatural. The fact that men and women of flesh and blood choose not to believe in Him cannot and will not, however, alter the bare facts that Almighty God reigns for ever.

Where are those who claim there is no God? Who are those who deny the Supernatural realm of our existence? Yes, where are those going about spreading the lie that life evolved from nowhere? Indeed, who are those propagating the concept of a universe coming about without a Creator? And where are the challengers to the power and authority of the Divine in our day? Let them stand up and be counted if they dare.

Fellow Christian soldiers battling diseases of various kinds, I join you in prayer to Glorious Jesus to implore Him to stretch His healing Hands over your body and restore your health—not to our glory, but to His own honour. May His name praised and glorified.

January 25

****

I am the resurrection, and the life. He that believeth in me, though he were dead, yet shall he live and whoever liveth and believeth in me shall never die.

– John 11:25 - 26

****

You who are mourning your loved one, from whose eyes the tears are so freely flowing, In a moment like this you may want to be left alone to wrestle with your sorrows alone, far from the presence of any human being. Still, I wish to express my heartfelt condolence and assure you that you are not alone in your difficult hour. Yes, the unseen Companion in whom you have placed your trust is by your side! Listen to Him as He whispers into your ears: 'I am the resurrection and the life – he who believes in me shall never die.'

You who are devastated by the sudden loss of a dear one: In moments like this we are tempted to question the Love of the Lord and wonder why the Loving one would allow such sorrow to visit our home. Christian friend, I have not come to provide suitable answers to your why's but I have come to urge you in the Name of the Lord of Heaven and Earth, in the Name of the Faithful One who called you out of the dark into light, yes, in the Name of Him whose Peace passeth all human understanding, to dry your tears and not be overcome by grief.

You who are grieving the departure of a loved one, I pray the Divine Comforter to send His angels to your home to sing a heavenly melody to cheer you up and revive your downcast spirit. May the great Comforter send a beam of light to dissipate the deep darkness surrounding you that you may be enabled to behold the Lord standing by the empty tomb of Calvary. So weep not like one without hope, dear one, for all who place their trust in Him, death has evermore been defeated!

January 26

****

And ye shall know the truth, and the truth shall make you free.

– John 8:32

****

As far as our Christian calling goes, truth is the unadulterated word of God and not what is thought , for example by human institutions – no matter how well respected .

Much as we should listen to the teachings of men and women of God, the bottom-line is that the Word of God is the final arbiter in spiritual matters.

Reading through the Gospels, my own layman's view is that the common sense the Lord has placed at our disposal aided by the working of the Holy Spirit is sufficient to lead us to a reasonably good understanding of the word of God, an understanding that should be enough to help us lead lives expected of our Holy calling.

The other day, I heard a pastor in my native Ghana teaching on radio that even children are required to pay tithes out of the pocket monies they receive from their parents (if any). Another church , attended mainly by natives of my country of birth was asking their members to pay tithe out of the child benefit they were receiving from the German welfare state system!

I may be wrong, but my common sense tells me that such an interpretation of scripture amounts to overstepping the rules, yes to putting unnecessary burdens on the sons and daughters of Precious Jesus.

Let us pray , fellow Christian soldier , for wisdom, yes pure wisdom from the source of all wisdom—wisdom that will, among others, enable us differentiate truth from falsehood in the interpretation of His Word.

January 27

****

The heart *is* deceitful above all *things*, and desperately wicked: who can know it?

– Jeremiah 17:9

****

The heart of man is wicked and wicked and wicked. In 1995, then a student in Hanover, I visited a friend also a student. He handed me printout of fresh news he had received from Ghana?

"From where did you get such first-hand report about things happening in Ghana?" I inquired.

"The internet." Was his reply.

"The internet ; what is that? "

Well it is an interconnection of computers. We resort to it a lot in the engineering department. Among other things , I get access to research material.

Shortly after the meeting I made my first contact with the internet. Soon I set up my first e-mail account.

The internet, what a great invention.

Without it, I wouldn't, be engaged in this my online ministry.

As in all aspects of life on a fallen planet, soon the sinful heart of man also discovered the internet.

The heart is deceitful above all things, and desperately wicked: who can know it?

Yes indeed, the same heart which built both the civilian plane and the fighter bomber, the same heart that invented nuclear power that can produce electricity for peaceful use and the nuclear bomb for human annihilation, yes indeed the same heart which can be as merciful as the Good Samaritan and as evil as Adolf Hitler also discovered the internet and with it online pornography, online terror, online spread of paedophile material!

Dear Christian soldiers, let us be vigilant, let us pray Almighty God to preserve ourselves, our children and the world at large from the evil side of the amazing internet.

May His name be blessed, Amen..

January 28

****

The LORD is merciful and gracious, slow to anger, and plenteous in mercy.

– Psalm 103:8

****

In 2009 the British Humanist association run an advert campaign to the theme: "There's probably no God. Now stop worrying and enjoy your life".

The inscription was printed boldly on buses, tube stations and other public places. I asked myself, then and ask myself today: what motivated them?

A closer look at the wording of their campaign led me also to the question: if they were very convinced in their assertion, why did they not leave it with the plain formulation– THERE IS NO GOD!

I also had issues with the phrase: " Now stop worrying and enjoy your life". The phrase created the false impression that those who believe in God, cannot enjoy life. Personally, I am happy and enjoying my life, so why did they want to speak on my behalf?

I do not know how much it cost for them to run the campaign. An article I read about the campaign had it that they managed to raise more than £140,000 through public donations.

It is worthy of note that one of their prominent supporters, a world-renowned Professor of science has in the meantime passed on.

I wish he could come back to life to realise how futile his attempt was, for even today, millions upon millions are still calling upon He who was yesterday, is today and shall evermore be!

My dear Christian friends, let's keep on praying for those who claim there is no God, that they may come out of spiritual blindness to behold the goodness of the Lord.

JANUARY 29

***

No weapon that is formed against thee shall prosper; and every tongue that shall rise against thee in judgment thou shalt condemn. This is the heritage of the servants of the Lord, and their righteousness is of me, saith the Lord.

– Isaiah 54:17

***

God Almighty, the creator of the whole universe—of the planets, the sun, the galaxies: yes everything seen and unseen—from the tiny bacteria to the huge whales of the ocean, from the mighty lion to the little mouse, from the beautiful roses to the thorns and thistles of the field, is assuring those who are seeking refuge in Him, that no weapons formed against them will prosper.

Yes indeed Almighty God who called the huge mountains, the vast oceans, the arid deserts etc. into existence, the King of Kings and Lord of Lords, the God Everlasting has signed a declaration from heaven promising to defend His children of from EVERY weapon directed against them!

To get even the faintest idea of what Almighty God is promising, let us imagine the tiny ant having the huge elephant for protection!

Let us picture the little and vulnerable mouse entering into a defence pact with the mighty and fierce lion, the lion guaranteeing the mouse a lifelong protection from his most dreaded enemy, the cat!

We might well consider the situation where a dollar billionaire from somewhere in our global village travels to an impoverished village in my native Ghana and picks up the most destitute child he/she spots playing on the street and declares in the presence of the whole world: "I swear by my honour, that I will make sure this little child never tastes poverty throughout the rest of his/her days on earth!!"

We have a more sure protection, from Almighty God, dear Christian friends so let's not fear tomorrow. Come what may, our protection is assured.

January 30

****

The angel of the LORD **encampeth round about them that fear him, and delivereth them.**

- Psalm 34:7

****

When I visited Johannesburg, South Africa, in February 2007, I realised that almost every house in the rich residential area boasted not only thick concrete walls; the properties were also equipped with sophisticated alarm systems. As if that were not enough—bold notices had been placed along the walls to warn the outside world that whoever attempted to break in would be met with a swift armed response.

Our modern world has come up with advanced high-tech alarm systems to help secure our homes from robbers. Even the most state-of-the-art alarm system, when activated, requires a certain amount of time for the appropriate response to be effected. For sure, no matter how swift the armed police or security officers may make it to the scene in response to the ringing of the alarm bells triggered by our advanced surveillance system, the intruders to our property would still have a few seconds at their disposal to cause us harm or escape as the case may be.

That, however, is not what the composer of Psalm 34 is declaring. He is pointing to protection offered by the angels of the living God to those who trust in Him, that is the powerful, all encompassing protection at the disposal of all who call on the Name of the Lord with a clean heart.

JANUARY 31

****
We are troubled on every side, yet not distressed; we are perplexed, but not in despair; Persecuted, but not forsaken; cast down, but not destroyed.

– 2 Corinthians 4:8-9
****

Dear fellow soldier of the Cross of Calvary, no matter the problem or problems confronting you, the problem or problems that is/are threatening to crush your body into minute, microscopic, pieces—from the crown of your head to the soles of your feet—rest assured that the Lord of Creation will surely respond to your cries; to your persistent calls for help!

You might as well despatch an e-mail, SMS, WhatsApp or whatever other forms of modern communication there are, to the camp of your enemies, your foes who are just about to clink their champagne glasses to celebrate what they think is your imminent demise, to tell them that the Lord of Creation will arise and fight on your behalf.

Indeed, help is coming; coming your way. Even should the seconds begin to tick towards zero; yes even just at the moment when the referee has begun the countdown: ten!, nine!, eight! seven!… even as you lie prostrate on your back at one corner of the ring, helpless and defenceless, the forces of darkness surrounding you on all sides, eagerly awaiting the "z-e-r-o" to issue from the throat of the referee, to fiercely pounce on you to tear your flesh apart; yes even apparent as defeat is staring you in the face, I still urge you not to be overcome by despair. Yes for sure , the Lord will intervene on your behalf to shame all those up against you!

February 1

****
And Joash said unto all that stood against him, Will ye plead for Baal? will ye save him? he that will plead for him, let him be put to death whilst it is yet morning: if he be a god, let him plead for himself, because one hath cast down his altar.

– Judges 6:31
****

We serve a living Jesus, who seeks to change hearts through love. He does not force Himself on anyone. In the face of provocation, he did not retaliate. While we may become upset by those who make mockery of His name, our protest should remain peaceful.

In this connection, I find it difficult to come to terms with the adherents of a religion, the name of which I do not want to mention here, who create the impression that they have to fight personally to defend their religion. When I see adherents of that religion on TV wielding swords and machetes, threatening to tear to pieces the bodies of those they regard as having insulted the dignity of their religion, I wonder why they feel the need to go to such lengths, resorting even to violence.

Why, at all, should ordinary humans create the impression of wanting to fight God's fight for Him? If Almighty God is supreme—and I am really convinced He is indeed—it is surely not up to me, common man of flesh who today is and tomorrow is, as it were, blown away with the wind, fight His fight for him. If He will sit down unconcerned whilst others take advantage of Him, so be it!

Dear fellow Christian soldiers, let's pray the Lord to imbue our hearts with abundant love and compassion, so we may be in a position to show affection and sympathy even in the face of provocation and insult.

February 2

Cast thy burden upon the Lord, and he shall sustain thee: he shall never suffer the righteous to be moved.

– Psalm 55:22

I wish sincerely, from the bottom of my heart, that Almighty God will spare us all the burdens and afflictions of life. Since we live in a fallen world there is no guarantee, however, that we shall always be spared trouble. How do we react in such a situation? As Christians, there is no other place to run to but to Christ our Lord. We must cultivate an attitude of looking up to Christ in all situations, whether good or bad. Easier said than done!

Indeed, how many headaches have we had to endure? How many anxious thoughts have threatened to blow our heads apart? Yes, in truth, how many distressing thoughts have robbed us of our sleep in anticipation of trouble that never showed up! Oh yes, how many problems have we borrowed today from tomorrow, from a tomorrow that may never arrive?

I have myself gone through times when anxious thoughts occupied my mind. Now, looking back on those periods in my life, I realise how pointless my state of apprehension was. Apart from causing me a few sleepless nights, it did not have any influence on the course of events.

Dear Christian friends, if only we would learn to put our burdens on the shoulders of the Lord instead of carrying them ourselves, how many problems that plague us—anxiety, tension headaches, sleep disturbance, depression—would be averted.

FEBRUARY 3

***

Fear thou not; for I am with thee: be not dismayed; for I am thy God: I will strengthen thee; yea, I will help thee; yea, I will uphold thee with the right hand of my righteousness.

– Isaiah 41:10

***

Once on a flight from Accra to Dusseldorf, we had been in the air for about two hours when an announcement was made to the effect that the Algerian authorities had refused us permission to enter their airspace so we were returning to Accra.

No one told us the reason behind the decision of the authorities of the North African country to deny us access to their air space. Eventually I got to know that it involved money—the airline had failed to settle a bill despite repeated calls on the them to do so.

So, after spending a total of about four hours in the air we returned to where we had set off—*back to square one!*

Are you going through your *back to square* one experience my dear Christian friend? Having done the required research with due diligence, you went for a loan to establish a business. You had put your best foot forward. You are indeed hardworking. You have made your very best effort—yet still no progress.

Whereas all your peers have settled down to start their families, your search for your future partner is not making any progress; you meet someone today who raises your hopes only for things to crash before your eyes a few weeks later—*back to square one*!

Don't resign yourself to your situation, my dear Christian friend.

"Back to square one" is by no means your destiny. It may be the Almighty God in whom you have trusted is just testing your resolve, just testing your faith and commitment to your call. One thing I can assure you, He will in His own time surely remove the obstacles that prevent you from realising your destiny. His message to you as you wait on Him is: "Fear thou not; for I am with thee: be not dismayed; for I am thy God: I will strengthen thee; yea, I will help thee; yea, I will uphold thee with the right hand of my righteousness."

February 4

****
From henceforth let no man trouble me: for I bear in my body the marks of the Lord Jesus.
– Galatians 6:17
****

Though the practice has been discontinued, at the time of my birth it was common practice for parents of the Akan population group to which I belong to inflict a cut to the face—on one or both cheeks—of their few-days-old babies. The wounds healed leaving a mark on the affected cheek(s). Such marks became known as tribal marks; marks that set a particular tribe aside from all others.

Today, as far as the Akans are concerned, the practice has virtually died away.

In later life some bearers of such marks, for various reasons, undertake efforts—including paying for cosmetic surgery—to rid themselves of the facial scar or scars as the case may be.

As I write this piece in 2018, though the tribal mark on my right cheek has grown faint, it is still visible. I have no intention of taking any measures aimed at getting rid of it.

St Paul in the above verse is said to have been referring to the scars resulting from the wounds inflicted on him in his service for the Lord.

I believe we can also refer to a "spiritual tribal mark", the Holy Spirit, that sets us apart from the other "tribes", indeed. which enables us not only to live Christ-like lives, but which also repels any attempt by the powers of darkness to inflict harm on us.

FEBRUARY 5

****
Therefore encourage one another and build each other up, just as in fact you are doing.

- 1 Thessalonians 5:11 (NIV)
****

Words of encouragement! Words that seek to uplift those facing troubles, problems and challenges of various kinds—how worthwhile. No matter our positions in society, no matter how strong we are in our Christian faith, we all need words of encouragement meant to motivate and inspire us in our life.

Conversely, consider how much derogatory words or comments can negatively impact on us. Several years ago, when I applied for Asylum in Berlin, I shared the same room with a few other Asylum seekers. I was desirous of studying medicine. The chances of gaining admission was not good. To have the faintest chance of my application being considered, I needed to show proof of my ability to speak the German language—which I could not do!

With no money to register at a German language school to learn the language, I was left with no other option than to attempt to do so on my own. Towards that goal I acquired a "Teach yourself German" book and went about the almost impossible task of teaching myself the new language. My room mates, instead of giving me words of encouragement to boost my morale, or at least remaining neutral, sought to discourage me with statements like: "Why waste your time learning this difficult language? No one would after all think of offering an Asylum seeker the chance to study at the Uni!" Had I listened to them, I would certainly not have achieved my goal.

Dear Christian friends, let us pray to the Lord for wisdom so we may find the right words, indeed, uplifting words, to build one another up instead of words that discourage us.

FEBRUARY 6

****
Train up a child in the way he should go: and when he is old, he will not depart from it.

- Proverbs 22:6
****

Sometimes, I begin to ponder over the mindset of humanity!
Let a person who yesterday was unknown to anyone, yes, whose character, whose trustworthiness has not been tested, excel as a footballer, athlete, a model, a film actor, and all of a sudden, that individual is catapulted into the limelight of the world.

Soon the world sees in them ROLE MODELS worthy of emulation by the youth!!

To be fair to the individuals involved, the office of Role Model was not of their own choosing. Some of them may well prefer to live quieter lives away from the limelight. They hardly succeed in doing so however; having imposed the roles on them, society goes to great lengths—welcome to Paparazzi land!—to ensure they remain on the centre-stage of our attention.

Dear Christian friends, as far as we are concerned there is one and only one Role Model, the Lord Jesus Christ. He alone should be our source of reference in all things. If we happen to be parents of young children, we should not be weary of directing them to the only role model worthy of their attention, the King of Kings and Lord of Lords.

February 7

****

David replied to the Philistine, You come to me with sword, spear, and javelin, but I come to you in the name of the Lord of Heaven's Armies—the God of the armies of Israel, whom you have defied.

– 1 Samuel 17:45

****

Dear Christian soldier, let us make the words of the shepherd boy David our battle cry.

For sure, on our own we are nothing before the enemy! Indeed, no matter what status we have achieved in our work for God on earth, the fact remains that on our own we are no match to the powers up against us.

On the contrary, as long as we abide in the Lord, we can with David declare to the forces against us—demons, principalities, juju power, voodoo power—that even though they may go to great lengths in their effort to destroy us and our family, our business, our reputation, we are not afraid or scared.

Yes indeed, whatever weapons they muster against us will not harm or hurt us!

FEBRUARY 8

****
For his anger endureth but a moment; in his favour is life: weeping may endure for a night, but joy cometh in the morning.

– Psalm 30:5
****

Fellow Christian soldier, you seem to see no way out in a seemingly dead-end situation.
To the right and to the left the storms have gathered;
behind you and in front the enemy is closing in!
You have prayed and fasted, fasted and prayed;
and once more prayed and fasted!
Yet an answer to prayer seems not forthcoming.
Doubt has begun to linger in your mind…
If He is so loving, why does He seem not to care?
If He is so omnipotent, why cannot I sense His presence?
If He is so powerful, why does He not display His might in my situation?
Hope indeed has given in to despair…
Still, I want to assure you: God is near when He seems very distant.
He is indeed a faithful Friend in whom we can rely!
So keep fighting the good fight until the day arrives
when the choir of Heaven descends on your home
to fill it with sweet heavenly melody.
Weeping may indeed endure for a night;
joy with all certainty cometh in the morning.
So cheer up, fellow Christian warrior, and keep marching on!

February 9

****

It is better to trust in the Lord than to put confidence in princes.

– Psalm 118:9

****

I have on several occasions placed my hope in flesh only to be disappointed. I am not pointing a finger of blame at anyone—that is simply human nature. You may be expecting someone to help you out of your woes; what you may not be aware of is that the individual concerned may also be in the hot soup!

In my culture family members are expected to help one another. The widespread poverty and the fact that, as of now, there is virtually no state benefit system in place to cater for those in need, has made family members tend to rely on each other all the more.

Through the mysterious workings of the Lord, I managed to make it all the way from my impoverished little village to medical school in Germany.

The fact that I am a medical doctor combined with the fact that I am currently resident in Europe, a place regarded by many at home as a kind of heaven on earth, has raised the expectations of some of my kinsmen literally to the highest heavens. That I am an ordinary man of flesh, plagued with my own problems has not sunk in to everyone. My inability to fulfil such elevated expectations could lead to disappointment in others.

Dear fellow Christian soldiers, let us learn to put our trust in the Lord rather than in flesh. For I know no power in the universe capable of guaranteeing absolute security in the vicissitudes of life other than the Divine Shepherd. He has been tested and found faithful—always!

FEBRUARY 10

****

But those who hope in the LORD will renew their strength. They will soar on wings like eagles; they will run and not grow weary, they will walk and not be faint.

– Isaiah 40:31 (NIV)

****

Very uplifting and edifying words indeed. For the Christian there is indeed no *cul-de-sac* or dead-end street. I personally can testify to that. There have indeed been a good number of instances in my life when it appeared to me as if I had reached the end of my road—indeed, that there was no way ahead for me to tread.

Today's Bible verse states that those "who hope in the Lord will renew their strength". The Lord who parted the Red Sea for His children to walk on dry ground is ever willing to intervene on behalf of His children—to create a way for them where there is no way.

The verse also declares that those who hope in the Lord "will soar on wings like eagles".

We are assured that when push comes to shove, yes indeed when our situation becomes critical, when the situation deteriorates, when we become hard pressed, indeed when we are confronted in a very narrow alley by the enemy, a red hot and glowing sword drawn, his eyes as red as crimson, literally sparking wrath and hatred—even in such critical moments let us not give up, for 'ere the destroyer attempts to strike us, yes, 'ere the foe strikes to inflict harm, angels will appear from nowhere to whisk us to safety!

February 11

****

Of old hast thou laid the foundation of the earth: and the heavens are the work of thy hands. They shall perish, but thou shalt endure: yea, all of them shall wax old like a garment; as a vesture shalt thou change them, and they shall be changed: But thou art the same, and thy years shall have no end.

– **Psalm 102:25-27**

****

Recent developments in the world political stage has strengthened my conviction, that if there is anything one can bank on, it is indeed only the Rock of Ages.

I have been on planet earth around six decades. My impression can be summed up thus—what an unstable world we live in!

When I was growing up, the Cold War between the East and West was at its climax.

Then came the collapse of the Eastern block of communist states.

I thought the Western block was built on more solid foundations so could survive the test of time. Maybe I was naive to think so.

Now as I write in the year 2018, cracks—yes, obvious cracks have started developing.

I am not a prophet of doom, but from the look of things it could be a matter of time when the Western block of countries as it used to be gives way to "something else".

Yes indeed, everything man-made is momentary, yes transitory. If ever there is any sure Foundation to build on, yes to hold on to, then it is indeed the Rock of Ages, the Ancient of Days, the Lord God.

February 12

****

Be strong and of a good courage, fear not, nor be afraid of them: for the Lord thy God, he it is that doth go with thee; he will not fail thee, nor forsake thee.

– Deuteronomy 31:6

****

What soothing words! We are assured of Divine company as we go about our daily activities. Our Lord is leading the way, so we need not worry.

We are like little schoolchildren on the way to school in the heart of a busy city the likes of New York, Tokyo, Peking—you name them. Left alone on the busy street, we face danger from various sides—vehicles of all sizes, motorbikes, evil men and women who may want to kidnap us for whatever reason, etc.

We are indeed like little chickens exposed to threats from hawks; like deer in the wild exposed to threats from lions.

Dear Christian soldier, as you go about your activities this day, do not fear evil, for indeed our Heaven Father is with us. 'Ere even the journey began, He had already dispatched His angels ahead to rid our path of spiritual landmines and other explosive devices planted on the way by the enemy. Even if Satan and His army should consider those threats as inadequate and decide to discharge troops to ambush us on the way, with the Lord by our side we need not fear.

February 13

Jesus saith unto her, Woman, believe me, the hour cometh, when ye shall neither in this mountain, nor yet at Jerusalem, worship the Father.

– John 4:21

After I have confessed my Christian faith, the question that usually follows is: Which church do you belong to?

I must say I personally do not feel comfortable with such a question. Ideally, the answer should be, "I belong to the Church of Jesus Christ My Lord!"

Our human imperfection has led to the denominations and churches too numerous to count, but based on the Lord's answer to the woman of Samaria, the Church of Jesus Christ is in the heart of the believer and not in church buildings.

I once had the following conversation with the caretaker of a large complex of premises boasting several small halls in Dusseldorf, Germany, where several different adherents of churches of the Ghanaian community worshipped.

"I have rented my premises to several small church groups from your country. Well, I am profiting from them. I do ask myself though—since they are worshipping the same Lord, why don't they unite and worship together as a single church and save money?"

I reflected over the matter. Whilst profiting financially from the fragmentation of the churches, indeed the disunity of the Christians, his own conscience had told him something was not in order.

Dear fellow Christian soldier, let us join hands and pray for Church unity, for at the end of the day we are worshiping our Loving Father through Jesus Christ our Lord. May the Holy Spirit help us overcome our division.

FEBRUARY 14

****
God is a spirit ; and they that worship Him must worship Him in spirit and in truth.

John 4:24
****

There is a terminology in my native Twi language—*Akwasi Amankwaa kristosom*. It refers to those who are Christians by name and not in deed.

God is a supernatural being, omnipotent and omnipresent—which means he is everywhere. The Lord we serve is a spirit. A spirit is like the air around us. So, we are called to hold high the flag of our calling wherever we are.

Christianity is not a 'show' religion, it permeates the heart. We are called upon to let our light shine not only when our pastors are present; not only on Sundays when we gather in our various churches to worship the Lord, be Christian, only on Sundays.

We should indeed strive to live by the tenets of our high calling. Though we are saved by grace, we should be careful not to take advantage of the kindness of our Lord.

Whatever we do today we are advised to keep in mind the words of our Lord—

> *Not everyone that saith unto me, Lord, Lord, shall enter into the kingdom of heaven; but he that doeth the will of my Father which is in heaven.*
>
> *Many will say to me in that day, Lord, Lord, have we not prophesied in thy name? and in thy name have cast out devils? and in thy name done many wonderful works?*
>
> *And then will I profess unto them, I never knew you: depart from me, ye that work iniquity.*
>
> Matthew 7:21-23 (KJV)

February 15

****

But Jesus called them unto him, and said, Suffer little children to come unto me, and forbid them not: for of such is the kingdom of God. Verily I say unto you, Whosoever shall not receive the kingdom of God as a little child shall in no wise enter therein.

– Luke 18:16 & 17

****

I read the following inspiring piece from *Great Texts of the Bible* by James Hastings—

"Signor Prochet, of the Waldensian Church, tells a story of a long-continued drought in the valleys of North Italy, which threatened to ruin the harvest. The pastor of one of the little congregations arranged to hold a special prayer-meeting to pray for rain to save the crops, and on the day of the meeting groups of people were seen wending their way along the valley, or clambering down the steep hillsides, to join the devotions.

As the minister was nearing the church a little girl passed him. He was much struck by the size of the umbrella she was carrying, and laughingly called out: "I fear you will not have much need of your umbrella in this weather." "Oh, sir," replied the child, "I brought it because we were going to ask God for rain today, and I will be sure to need it before I get home." The minister pondered the words, and rebuked himself for his lack of faith.

He had been going to pray for rain, but without any expectation that his prayer would be answered. The faith of the child put new life and power into the prayer-meeting. Before the close there was a sound of abundance of rain, and the minister was glad to share the shelter of the big umbrella on his way home."

Dear Christian friend, if you have been praying for blessings to pour on your home, do believe, like that little girl, and get ready for your miracle—in Jesus Name, Amen!

February 16

****

Thou shalt not be afraid for the terror by night; nor for the arrow that flieth by day; Nor for the pestilence that walketh in darkness; nor for the destruction that wasteth at noonday. A thousand shall fall at thy side, and ten thousand at thy right hand; but it shall not come nigh thee. Only with thine eyes shalt thou behold and see the reward of the wicked.

– Psalm 91:5-8

****

Those who grew up with electricity may not be able to appreciate how dark it can be at night.

When I was growing up in my little village, we did not have access to electricity. It turned very dark in the night, yes, deep, deep dark.

Even before we retired to bed, I was scared to move too far away from the Swiss kerosene lamp that provided us with light.

One could imagine how scary it was when one needed to get out in the middle of the night—to follow the call of nature for example. On stepping out of the room, one was greeted by utter darkness.

Our house was the first to be built on our part of the street. There was no fence or wall around it; it was bordered directly by bush. Sometimes when I stepped out, out of fear, it appeared to me as if I could see some shadowy figures, perhaps ghosts, walking in the dark, even threatening to pounce on me. If it happened a resident of the little settlement in which each one knew the other had recently passed away, the thought of a face-to-face confrontation with the dead person aggravated my fear.

My terror by night was without doubt enhanced by a vivid imagination. The Bible speaks of terror by night as well as pestilence that 'walketh in darkness'—the principalities and demonic powers—that are real and not imagined. Without Divine protection, the children of God are no match against them.

One would have thought that our enemies would limit their attacks to the cover of darkness; but no, destruction 'wasteth also at day'.

Having failed to inflict damage on us in the dark, Satan and a host of demons will not give up the pursuit. Yes, they also pursue us in broad daylight. Indeed the powers against us won't spare any opportunity at getting at us!

Nevertheless, dear Christian friend, let us not worry, for Divine protection is forever assured.

February 17

****

The LORD is thy keeper: the LORD is thy shade upon thy right hand.

The sun shall not smite thee by day, nor the moon by night.

The LORD shall preserve thee from all evil: he shall preserve thy soul.

The LORD shall preserve thy going out and thy coming in from this time forth, and even for evermore.

– Psalm 121:5-8

****

As I was busy at work on my laptop, all of us sudden, without prior warning, the screen turned blue and blank. Soon the notice "Your Computer Has Encountered a Problem and Needs to Restart" flashed on the screen.

I began to reflect on the incident. Whilst I was at work, viruses and malwares of various types and sources were attempting to infiltrate my laptop to destroy it. While I was unaware of what was happening, the virus protector had confronted the danger and dealt it a knockout blow. To make sure everything was back to normal, the system had to re-start.

Children of Almighty God also face constant threats from the enemy.

In the same way that the virus protector is at work to shield our computer from attack from viruses, our Lord is at work in the background warding off one demonic attack after the other, attacks directed not only at us but also at our family, business and everything associated with us.

Whereas even the best virus protector around can from time to time be outwitted by the attackers, we have a sure defender, He who is able to offer protection beyond what is needed.

How comforting, my dear Christian friends, the thought that we are guaranteed around-the-clock Divine protection.

FEBRUARY 18

****
Even though I walk through the valley of the shadow of death, I fear no evil, for You are with me; Your rod and Your staff, they comfort me.

– Psalm 23:4
****

After switching on my laptop early in the morning of Sunday December 1, 2018, as was my custom, I decided to check the BBC Online News to update myself of the latest happenings in the world: **George Bush Senior dies at the age of 94,** I was confronted with this headline.

Reading through the news, I got to know that he passed away at 22:10 hrs local time on Friday November 29. Of course, he was not the only person to have passed away on that day, but for obvious reasons, his passing away was made headline news the world over. It was not his fault that he had met the ultimate fate of mortal man. He who created us had ordained it and so it must happen. The fact of his passing brought the fact of my own mortality powerfully home to me.

As soldiers of the cross, we need not fear the confrontation with the ultimate, however, for the Lord we serve has indeed overcome the enemy. "I am the resurrection and the life. He who believes in Me, though he may die, he shall live. And whoever lives and believes in Me shall never die." He declared this at the grave of Lazarus.

Let us go into the world, fellow Christian soldiers, and proclaim the Good News at the top of our voices!

February 19

****
Now then we are ambassadors for Christ, as though God did beseech you by us: we pray you in Christ's stead, be ye reconciled to God.

– 2 Corinthians 5:20
****

We are indeed ambassadors, though not worldly ambassadors of our respective countries, but ambassadors of the Good Shepherd.

Renowned citizens of countries help raise the profiles of their respective countries of origin.

Let an athlete, a footballer, a boxer, etc., from an unknown country of the earth excel on the world stage, at the Olympic Games for example, and for once the world takes notice of his or her country of origin. Those who until then had not heard the name of the country involved may search online for the location of the country on the world map or look out for it in the atlases on their bookshelves.

When the late Kofi Annan was sworn in as the seventh UN Secretary General in January 1997, I was residing in Germany. Aware that I happened also to be from Ghana, over the next several days, my German friends, working colleagues, acquaintances, etc., never lost the opportunity to raise the issue in our conversations and express their best wishes for him.

His appointment, without doubt, led many who previously had not heard about my country of birth to look out for its location on the map.

We are ambassadors, not of worldly nations that may not withstand the tide of time; we are ambassadors of the eternal King of Kings and Lord of Lords. We have a very high calling, my fellow Christian soldiers. Let us, in all that we do—at home, at school, at work, in politics—make a difference; yes, let our light so shine before men, that they may see our good works, and glorify our Father which is in heaven (Matthew 5:16 KJV).

FEBRUARY 20

****
For my thoughts are not your thoughts, neither are your ways my ways, saith the Lord. For as the heavens are higher than the earth, so are my ways higher than your ways, and my thoughts than your thoughts.

– Isaiah 55:8-9
****

One of the most important lessons I have learnt since I made a conscious decision to following the Lord can be summed up as follows: Man proposes, but God disposes.

I dare even assert that if you have indeed left everything to follow the Lord you better *even stop* making plans for the future!!

I hear you say: "How dare you say that! We do indeed need to make plans for the future."

Well, I better modify my statement a bit. We do indeed have to plan for tomorrow! We need, however, to qualify any aspirations or intentions we have for the future with the words IF HE SO WILLS IT!

I am saying so out of personal experience, friend. Indeed, I can cite several instances in my life where the plans of the Divine have crossed my own. I would like to cite an example from my own life.

At the time of my conversion in September, 1978, my own plans for the future were as follows:

I was hoping to pass well in the General Certificate of Education (GCE) A-levels exams which I had sat a few weeks before (the results were still pending) and be admitted to one of the two medical schools in the country at that time. Based on my own plans, I would have entered medical school in the 1978/79 academic year and passed out six years later in June 1985.

That I would end up studying medicine, not in Ghana, but in Germany, not by way of an easy path—for example by virtue of a

Ghana government Scholarship—but rather by way of a difficult and uncertain path that went through Nigeria, East Germany, West Berlin and finally Hanover—was something I had never envisaged. In the end I began my studies in October 1984 six years later than I had thought!

February 21

But the God of all grace, who hath called us unto his eternal glory by Christ Jesus, after that ye have suffered a while, make you perfect, stablish, strengthen, settle you.

– 1 Peter 5:10

From my own personal Christian experience, I have come to the conclusion that it is very important we make it clear to the new convert of the FAITH that having decided to follow the Lord does not mean he or she will be excluded from suffering.

Instead, it is helpful to point out to such "infants" in the faith that everyone's Christian experience is different.

Someone may indeed experience a rosy path devoid completely or almost completely of troubles. It is also true that for some, the path may be bumpy, indeed not devoid of considerable amount of suffering.

We can nevertheless take consolation from the fact that the Christian path ahead is not all valleys, not all suffering, for indeed the saying is true that we will not be permitted to suffer beyond what we can bear.

Indeed it is true that for those of us who have to go through trials and difficulties, after we have suffered a little while, the Lord himself will restore us and make us strong, firm and steadfast.

February 22

And base things of the world, and things which are despised, hath God chosen, yea, and things which are not, to bring to nought things that are.

– 1 Corinthians 1:28

Fellow Christian soldier, the world may count you the least amongst your fellow human beings—not counted among the wealthy, the influential, the prominent; neither among the educated nor the political elite.

You may, like myself, have been born into abject poverty; indeed, as in my case, a makeshift bathroom in one of the most impoverished areas on the globe might have served as the delivery suite where your eyes first saw the light of day!

Today's verse does not, in any case, exclude the fact that the Lord also uses those of noble birth or standing. Certainly, He has in the past used them and will in the future also use any of a high social standing who open up to Him.

The fact still remains though that Almighty God is not impressed by outside appearances. Indeed, He is ever willing to use not only those at the top rung of the social ladder, but those of the lowest as well.

February 23

****

Be anxious for nothing, but in everything by prayer and supplication, with thanksgiving, let your requests be made known to God; and the peace of God, which surpasses all understanding, will guard your hearts and minds through Christ Jesus.

– Philippians 4:6-7 (NKJV)

****

What are you facing today, dear friend? Is it poverty? I have also known poverty, material poverty. Yes, I was born into poverty, yes, I experienced the worst form of poverty and deprivation. Not that I am today swimming in riches. By His grace though I am supplied with the basic necessities of life.

Are you unemployed, or threatened with joblessness? I have also faced it. At one stage during my medical training in Germany, I was for a while jobless because I was denied the necessary paperwork to enable me to work. As a doctor with a foreign passport, I did not fulfil the criteria required for the issuance of a work permit to enable me do my post-graduate training. In the end the Lord literally created a way where there was no way.

Are you facing ill-health, a condition threatening to disrupt your plans? When I got to Year 5 in Primary School, an ailment to my left ankle forced an interruption in my education for two good years!

Just when the whole world seemed to have given up on me the Lord restored me to good health and enabled me to resume my education.

No matter the problem facing you, I urge you Christian soldier, not to give up, not to throw in the towel, but instead to keep on hoping against hope, until heaven dispatches the long-awaited e-mail to announce the end of your woes.

FEBRUARY 24

****

And thou shalt love the Lord thy God with all thy heart, and with all thy soul, and with all thy mind, and with all thy strength: this is the first commandment. And the second is like, namely this, Thou shalt love thy neighbour as thyself. There is none other commandment greater than these.

– **Mark 12:30-31**

****

After graduation from medical school in Germany, I sought for placement as a junior doctor in a hospital as part of my specialisation. It was a time when there was an overproduction of junior doctors in the system. With the available placement vacancies limited, competition was tough.

I sent one application after the other only to be met with one rejection letter after the other.

Finally, one day, I received a letter from a hospital requesting me to attend an interview.

On the appointed day, I left home early for the approximately 70-kilometre drive. In the end I got to my destination about forty-five minute ahead of time. After reporting to the administration, I was asked to wait in an adjacent room till I was called.

A few minutes after taking my seat, the door opened; in stepped a nicely dressed lady of about my age. The expression on her face betrayed a feeling of nervousness. She greeted me politely and took her seat.

"I am here for an interview, I am really anxious," she began after a short while.

"You are here for an interview?"

"Yes"

"For which job?"

"Junior doctor in General Surgery."

"That is the very reason why I am also here!"

"In that case we are direct competitors!" she replied, a broad smile on her face. "Let's keep our fingers crossed for each other," she continued.

"I will rather pray for you!" I replied.

Not long thereafter, she was called for her interview.

"Praying for the person you are competing with for the same job!" I said to myself and began to laugh at myself!

About half an hour after she was called it came to my turn. I did not see her again. I did not get the job and I wonder if she did.

I do not remember if I specifically prayed for her. What I remember is that I did not harbour any ill feelings towards her—I only prayed for the will of the Lord to be done in my life.

Dear fellow soldiers of the Cross, when faced with challenging situations, pray to our Heaven Father for the wisdom to act in line with His will.

FEBRUARY 25

****

Fear thou not; for I am with thee: be not dismayed; for I am thy God: I will strengthen thee; yea, I will help thee; yea, I will uphold thee with the right hand of my righteousness.

– Isaiah 41:10

****

When we board a plane, we put our faith in the pilot to fly us safely to our destination. On very few occasions things do not go as expected, leading to unexpected outcomes, indeed in some cases catastrophes. In the overwhelming majority of cases, however, the pilot and his crew indeed get us to our destination.

Well, my dear Christian friend, we have Captain Jesus at the helm of our flight to the Promised Land so we need not worry.

Are a swarm of birds heading towards the engine, possibly to cause danger to the flight? Remain calm, my friend and do not panic.

Just as the danger from the birds is over and you have climbed thousands of feet above sea level, one of the engines is reported to be malfunctioning, so you are making an emergency landing.

Just as the plane is making a swift descent, an announcement to the effect that the remaining engine also appears to be faulty!

As if all the problems besetting your ill-fated flight is not enough, the plane encounters severe turbulence!

No need for panic, my dear Christian warrior, no need for hysteria. Yes, I urge you to keep calm, for all will be well, all will be well.

Indeed, should your plane take a nosedive into the deep ocean below, 'ere it hits the bottom of the ocean, angels of heaven will be dispatched to whisk you to your heavenly home!

February 26

****

Be patient therefore, brethren, unto the coming of the Lord. Behold, the husbandman waiteth for the precious fruit of the earth, and hath long patience for it, until he receive the early and latter rain. Be ye also patient; stablish your hearts: for the coming of the Lord draweth nigh.

– James 5:7-8

****

I read the story of a bus driver in the UK who on reaching a bus stop mistook the accelerator for the break, causing a crash which in turn resulted in two deaths and several injuries, not to mention the material damage. My thoughts are with the family and friends of the casualties.

This is not the only instance of drivers mistaking the break for the accelerator I have heard of. Though not all instances led to a tragedy similar to the one described, it is no doubt a mistake that is a nightmare for any driver.

What is true in the physical world is also true of the spiritual, indeed of our walk with the Lord. We are all inclined to get things done quickly, to attain quick results. I am not implying that it is wrong to get things done as quickly as we can. In matters relating to our Christian walk, things may not always proceed as quickly as we wish.

Moses had to undergo 40 years of training before being considered fit for the huge task meant for him. In the same way, we may indeed have to wait for the Lord to prepare us adequately for service, indeed to be able to cope with the challenges of the tasks assigned for us.

Dear Christian soldiers, let's pray to the Lord for patience and steadfastness as we await His will to be manifested in our lives.

FEBRUARY 27

****
I will not cause pain without allowing something new to be born, says the Lord.

– Isaiah 66:9
****

I was privileged to witness the birth of a baby as a second-year medical student doing my electives at a district hospital in a little town not far from Hanover, the northern German city where I was resident. For the first time in my life I witnessed at first hand a woman in labour—a soon-to-be mother enduring the pain, indeed the intense pain, of childbirth.

What I observed shortly after the beautiful little girl who was christened Ina was delivered is engraved deeply in my memory. Indeed, the moment the new mother looked upon the little new arrival placed on her bosom, she beamed with joy at the sight of her wonderful baby. Vanished in a twinkle of the eye was the agony, yes, the pain that was evident in her face moments before as she pushed, and pushed hard to deliver her lovely baby.

Child of God going through intense affliction and sorrow, I cannot explain why our loving Father has allowed misfortune to visit your home. I do indeed wish from the bottom of my heart, that you are spared the anguish of new challenges.

Who am I, a man of flesh, to determine the course of events in your life? One thing I can do, however, is to urge you to take comfort in today's Bible verse. Indeed, our heavenly Father "will not cause pain without allowing something new to be born."

May the pain of today usher you into the joy of tomorrow.

FEBRUARY 28

****

Jesus saith unto her, Woman, believe me, the hour cometh, when ye shall neither in this mountain, nor yet at Jerusalem, worship the Father. Ye worship ye know not what: we know what we worship: for salvation is of the Jews. But the hour cometh, and now is, when the true worshippers shall worship the Father in spirit and in truth: for the Father seeketh such to worship him. God is a Spirit: and they that worship him must worship him in spirit and in truth.

– John 4:21-24

****

I learnt during my stay in Germany that at the height of World War II it was customary for residents to seek protection in church buildings. Seeking protection in such places of worship did not always spare those sheltering there from attack. Indeed, in some instances all or most of them sheltering there perished in bombing raids.

It is said that as a result of that experience many lost their faith. "If there is a God, why did He not protect those seeking shelter in places where Christians gather to worship Him?" some are said to have stated in disgust.

My heart goes out to all who lost their lives in that terrible epoch of history.

Our Lord Jesus Christ pointed out to the woman of Samaria that it is a misconception to think that Almighty God resides in buildings or other places of worship.

We do of course gather in church buildings to worship Him, but that does not mean He resides in them! Since the advent of the Holy Spirit, God's spirit dwells in us, not in church buildings!

FEBRUARY 29

****

Blessed be God, even the Father of our Lord Jesus Christ, the Father of mercies, and the God of all comfort; Who comforteth us in all our tribulation, that we may be able to comfort them which are in any trouble, by the comfort wherewith we ourselves are comforted of God.

– 2 Corinthians 1:3-4

****

Have mercy Lord on your children who are
tired and weary;
who in the face of the fierce battle raging
are on the verge of throwing in the towel;
'Ere we give up the righteous fight,
imbue us we pray with new vigour.

Have mercy on your children Lord
your children who are panicking,
who in the midst of the ferocious spiritual battle raging
are relying on their own strength for victory
instead of in You.
Have mercy on your sheep, Divine Shepherd,
Your servants who in the midst of the fearsome
fight raging
seem to have lost sight of the most effective weapon at
our disposal—prayer!
Yes, teach us to bring all our cares and burdens before
you in prayer instead of grieving your heart with our
murmurings!

March 1

****

But I say unto you, Love your enemies, bless them that curse you, do good to them that hate you, and pray for them which despitefully use you, and persecute you;
   That ye may be the children of your Father which is in heaven: for he maketh his sun to rise on the evil and on the good, and sendeth rain on the just and on the unjust.
– **Matthew 5:44-45**

****

We need to be grateful to Almighty God for the air we breathe.

Yes for sure, no matter the challenges we are confronted with, let us at least be grateful to Almighty God for the free oxygen at our disposal.

Let us for a minute pause and consider a hypothetical situation where we are required to purchase the daily supply of oxygen required to ventilate our lungs! Let us indeed assume that humanity has control over the supply of air, yes, that it is traded on the stock market—London, Tokyo, New York, you can keep on naming them! Do you think anyone would show you mercy if you had no means to purchase a supply?

There is a saying in my mother tongue that he who has no idea of death, should consider sleep. Based on current politics and market mechanisms appertaining to food and water, greedy man would have watched unconcerned as others died for lack of money to purchase the life-saving air!

Instead of Mankind worshiping Almighty God from the rising of the sun to its setting for the free air at our disposal, we, by our nature, keep on spitting in His face.

So fellow Christian soldiers, whatever the problem we are going through, let us not murmur and be angry with Almighty God. Let us instead be grateful for at least the air we are privileged to breathe free of charge!

MARCH 2

And be not drunk with wine, wherein is excess; but be filled with the Spirit.

– Ephesians 5:18

Sometimes, when alone, I try to recall some of the things I did when I was a child. One of such childhood behaviours led me to laugh my guts out! Indeed, during those days, when I was angry with my parents, I sought to retaliate by refusing to eat for a while. Yes, the poor deluded boy went on a kind of hunger strike, thinking that by refusing to eat he would somehow be punishing his parents!

When scripture advises mankind to turn from our sins and follow the Lord, we seem to think that Almighty God is bossy, yes, trying to put this and that impediment in our way.

Today scripture urges us not to "be drunk with wine, wherein is excess; but be filled with the Spirit."

Excellent advice! In this age of the internet when one can read about virtually everything, one does not necessarily have to be in the health-care profession to acquire a fairly good knowledge concerning the harm alcohol can inflict on various organs of the body—the liver, the pancreas, the brain, the heart, etc.

Apart from directly affecting the organs of the body, alcohol no doubt can ruin relationships, lead to crime, yes even to imprisonment.

The other day, I even read about a young student who drank so much alcohol within a short period of time that his body was literally poisoned by alcohol, leading to his untimely death.

Dear Christian soldier, let us cherish our freedom, and not subject ourselves again to the yoke of slavery.

March 3

****

And at midnight Paul and Silas prayed, and sang praises unto God: and the prisoners heard them. And suddenly there was a great earthquake, so that the foundations of the prison were shaken: and immediately all the doors were opened, and every one's bands were loosed

– Acts 16:25-34

****

Do you have the feeling that you have been imprisoned by the powers that be in this world? Does it feel as if you are a prisoner in chains?

Since you made a decision to follow the Lord, nothing seems to be going well in your life. On the contrary, things have gone from bad to worse and ended up being the worst you could ever imagine!

Your business is not prospering, your relations with your spouse which used to be excellent seems to have hit rock-bottom.

And your children, they are not doing better. Their school grades are getting worse.

In your desperation, you are tempted to look elsewhere; yes, you are being tempted to seek help from palm readers, spiritualists, voodoo, juju, etc.

Indeed, you seem to be in a prison; not only are you incarcerated, you are also in chains. I urge you to draw inspiration from the suffering of Paul and Silas. Even as midnight approaches, yes, as the time ticks towards your possible execution by the powers of darkness, keep on singing and praising the Lord—for indeed the hand of heaven will shake the prison gate and set you free!

MARCH 4

****
But Jesus looked at them and said to them, 'With men this is impossible, but with God all things are possible.

– Matthew 19:26
****

The human mind, how limited it is! Much as the learned physicians of our day have tried, they have not been able to decipher exactly how the brain functions; we have not completely been able to do so. Indeed, the soft matter of the brain which the Creator placed in our skulls to help us among other things to reason and understand our environment, is itself incapable of understanding fully how it functions!

Just let us ponder over the matter for a moment: the brain itself is incapable of understanding, even to a hundred percent, the exact functions assigned to its individual parts.

Of course, over the years through research. a good deal of knowledge concerning the function of the brain has been acquired— yet the fact still remains that we have not been able to understand everything. Now, if our brain has not been able to understand itself, does it come as a surprise that we cannot understand the workings of Almighty God? Because the human mind is limited in its ability to comprehend everything around it, we seem to think we share the same weakness and restrictions with Almighty God.

Indeed, while our omnipotent God knows and sees all, present and future, we remain incapable of predicting exactly what the next few minutes have in store for us. Will the earth on which our homes are built quake to send us to our untimely death? Will the heart which has been dutifully pumping blood to keep us alive decide to switch off its battery and go to rest, sending us to our graves? Will a stray bullet of a shot fired for whatever reason penetrate our window and kill us instantly? Only God knows.

Yet in spite of our human limitations, you and I are inclined to place limitations on Almighty God!

Dear Christian soldiers, let us learn to bring our requests to the Lord and leave everything in the capable hands of He whose powers know no bounds!

MARCH 5

***

Come unto me all ye that labour and are heavy laden and I will give you rest.

– Matthew 11:25

***

Several countries in the Western industrialised world boast a generous welfare state. In times of need—unemployment, disease, threat of homelessness etc.— residents affected by these circumstances can look towards the state for financial and material assistance. In Germany the term *Vaterstaat*, standing literally for "the state is my father" has been coined to describe the quite generous welfare state system prevailing there.

The system, of course, functions only as long as the economy of the country is able to sustain it. A serious economic downturn could handicap the extent to which the state can help its needy residents, if not completely prevent it.

Whereas the man-made *Vaterstaat* can at best only provide its citizens material help, it is not able to make provisions for their spiritual needs. Thus, whereas residents may be fairly well provided for materially, many are spiritually empty, even plagued with depressions, anxiety, hopelessness, etc.

Almighty God offers a better *Vaterstaat*—a welfare state system which is not limited to our material well-being, but most importantly has our spiritual happiness at heart.

Come unto me all ye that labour and are heavy laden and I will give you rest—yes, a respite or sanctuary that no human system or institutions can offer.

Dear Christian friend, let us with all vigour and vitality carry the message of salvation to the world, indeed point the world to the Divine Shepherd who is ever willing to provide for both our material and spiritual needs.

March 6

****

No weapon forged against you will prevail, and you will refute every tongue that accuses you. This is the heritage of the servants of the Lord, and this is their vindication from me, declares the Lord.

– Isaiah 54:17

****

Once on a visit to my native Ghana, I began all of a sudden to experience a hot sensation my heart. Next it began to race as fast as one can imagine, as if it were engaged in a 100-metre race with the likes of Usain Bolt! Soon, I felt like "passing out"! *Lord Jesus, have mercy, Lord Jesus, Have mercy!* I prayed. A few minutes after it all began, things returned to normal without the need for me to seek medical intervention.

I thought that was the end of the matter! On my return to the UK a few days later, I was at work when I experienced a similar attack of my heart. I ended up being rushed to the Accident and Emergency, A&E. In one moment I was a doctor helping the sick, the next moment a patient at the A&E!

Over the next few days I underwent several checks on my heart, including a heart scan! In the end my heart was pronounced as "fit as a fiddle"!

Having ruled out an organic cause of my symptoms, it became clear to me that I was under attack by an evil entity. I decided therefore to charge on the enemy, not by my strength, but with the shield of faith for protection.

Yes, on stepping out of my doctor's premises, even as I walked on the street to pick my vehicle, I declared boldly: "Hey, you demons and principalities up against me, you better beware! Yes, you Philistines of the spiritual realm, you come to me with spears; I come to you in the Mighty Name of the Lord! I command you in the Mighty Name of the Lord to depart from me and go drown in the Mighty Ocean!"

Five years have elapsed since I launched that onslaught on the Demons. Not only has my heart been left in peace, nothing untoward has happened to my health.

Dear Christian soldiers, the Devil is indeed real, but we have an All-conquering God, so let us fear no foe.

March 7

****

For the Lord himself shall descend from heaven with a shout, with the voice of the archangel, and with the trump of God: and the dead in Christ shall rise first: Then we which are alive and remain shall be caught up together with them in the clouds, to meet the Lord in the air: and so shall we ever be with the Lord. Wherefore comfort one another with these words.

– 1 Thessalonians 4:16-18

****

In 2018, the effort of a citizen of Holland to get the authorities to officially recognize a reduction in his age made headline news. The individual concerned was requesting a 20-year reduction in his age! According to him he felt like a 49-year old instead of feeling like someone aged 69, his actual age. A very interesting character, one might describe him. I pray the Lord to bless him with more years. In particular I pray he may come to know the Lord, if he has not yet made the Great Redeemer his Saviour.

As soldiers of Christ, we need not be bothered with issues relating to age, for indeed as long as we abide in the Lord, we are "ageless", indeed immortal.

March 8

Even to your old age and gray hairs I am he, I am he who will sustain you. I have made you and I will carry you; I will sustain you and I will rescue you.

– Isaiah 46:4

I want to make one thing clear at the outset—what you are about to read is based on my own observation. Yes, what I am just about to write is not based on any scientific study, but rather based on my own observation. You may have a different opinion from mine, indeed you may have come to a different conclusion based on your own personal observation.

The observations that I make here are for the readers I am publishing these posts for and I appreciate that one cannot generalize. Based on my personal observation, I have come to realize how the Lord keeps His children young and vibrant!

In my work as a doctor, when I look at the DOBs of some of my patients, especially those whose lives have been taken over by drugs of various kinds, they tend to look far older than their actual age. I am not saying this is perfect science.

The Holy Spirit dwelling in us, freeing our minds from thoughts of jealousy, envy, malice, releases joy and happiness in our hearts; as a result our defence system is boosted, not only through prayer, but by a vibrant immune system. Indeed, *"Even to your old age and gray hairs I am he, I am he who will sustain you. I have made you and I will carry you; I will sustain you and I will rescue you."*

March 9

You are the salt of the earth.

– Matthew 5:13

As part of my medical training in Germany, I needed to do a one-year internship in the practice of a General Practitioner (GP) or a family doctor.

After submitting several applications and receiving several rejection letters, to my delight I finally received a letter inviting me for interview in a small town about 70 kilometres from Hanover. The General Practice concerned happened to be the only one in the little town. To my delight, my future boss assured me after the interview that he would take me on—we only needed to complete some paperwork related to the appointment.

Just as I was rejoicing at the opportunity, he called me a few days later to inform me that some members of the Practice team had expressed their reservation to the effect that the patients, who were predominantly German, may not be comfortable with me by dint of my African heritage. This was particularly so because it involved a rural population, most of whom had little or no dealings with Africans. I replied by saying that the final decision was his to make. On my part I would do my best if given the opportunity.

Over the following days, I prayed for the Lord to let his will be done. A few days later he called to confirm the job.

Apart from seeing patients in the practice, my duties included visiting those whose conditions prevented them from attending in the premises of the medical practise. This group included the few who were either living in old people's homes or at home, in some cases alone in their large mansions. Because they were socially isolated, for these people the visiting doctor would be the first person they would talk to the whole day! Whenever my tight schedule permitted, I stayed on a few minutes to engage them in conversation over various issues, including of course my faith. Indeed, for some of them just being friendly to them, talking to them, smiling with them, was the only "medicine" they needed.

From the conversation I had with my boss towards the end of my duty, it appeared that the majority of the patients I saw wished that I had stayed on, if not indefinitely, for at least a much longer period.

Unfortunately, I needed to move on. With a heavy heart, one day, I parted company with my wonderful boss, the excellent team and the downhearted patients.

We are indeed the salt of the earth, my dear friends, so wherever we go, let us make our influence be felt.

March 10

****
Brethren, I count not myself to have apprehended: but this one thing I do, forgetting those things which are behind, and reaching forth unto those things which are before, I press toward the mark for the prize of the high calling of God in Christ Jesus.

– Philippians 3:13-14
****

Dear Fellow Christians, let us like St Paul press forward; forward toward the goal for the prize of the upward call of God in Christ Jesus. Forward; yes, ahead is our only destination! Not backwards, but forward march, dear Christian friends.

Let us indeed resist the temptation to look back, to look behind and among other things regret our mistakes made, opportunities missed, poor decisions made, etc. What will we gain from weeping over spilt milk? Do we want to invest our precious time and energy to recover the polluted stuff, yes, the mess contaminated with billions if not trillions of bacteria and other microscopic organisms and gulp it down our throats?

Dear Christian soldiers, let us resist grieving the Spirit of our Master with our continual grieving over the past. Instead like apostle Paul let us forget things that are behind; let us forget past sorrows, the dark paths and low valleys of the past and join hands with Apostle Paul in pressing forward; yes, pressing ahead towards the goal for the prize of the upward call of God in Christ Jesus.

MARCH 11

***

The righteous cry, and the LORD heareth, and delivereth them out of all their troubles. The LORD is nigh unto them that are of a broken heart; and saveth such as be of a contrite spirit. Many are the afflictions of the righteous: but the LORD delivereth him out of them all.

– Psalm 34:17-19

***

My dear Christian soldier, whose soul is downcast in the face of the enormous problems confronting you, I pray Almighty God to help turn around your situation, just the same way He did in the case of Joseph.

Indeed, I want to convey to you, dear soldier of the cross of Calvary whose neck seems to be breaking under the sheer weight of burdens you are bearing, the message of hope and comfort. Whatever the problems confronting you, be assured that we serve a 'turn-around' God who will with all certainty turn your situation around.

Yes indeed, even should you be stuck on the upper floor of your home with fire raging all around you, to your left and to your right, upstairs and below, even though you are threatened with suffocation, even in that seemingly helpless situation, I want to assure you that we serve the only true God—He who has the power and authority to turn your situation around. He is indeed a very present help in time of trouble, so be of good cheer, embattled Christian soldier.

March 12

***

Thus saith the Lord, Let not the wise man glory in his wisdom, neither let the mighty man glory in his might, let not the rich man glory in his riches: But let him that glorieth glory in this, that he understandeth and knoweth me, that I am the Lord which exercise lovingkindness, judgment, and righteousness, in the earth: for in these things I delight, saith the Lord.

– Jeremiah 9:23-24

***

Fellow Christian soldiers, let us not allow the wisdom and ideas of men and women of letters to draw us away from what matters most—an unflinching faith in God. After all, what is man? He is but like the grass and flowers of the field that blossom today only to wither away tomorrow.

Fellow child of God, let us indeed not allow the wisdom and ideas of man to draw us away from what matters most—an unshakeable belief in God.

The world has in the past produced and even today continues to produce men and women of ideas—philosophers, experts, great thinkers, etc.

The ideas of the brilliant men and women of thought and letters have influenced the thinking of society and in some instances contributed to its progress.

The Christian is warned to be on guard in respect of ideas and thoughts emanating from mortal man that are at variance with Biblical teaching—however valid they may appear! We should indeed take them with a pinch of salt. Indeed, whenever the teachings of man contradict Divine principles, true wisdom requires that we hold on to those coming from Him that was true yesterday, true today and evermore shall be true.

March 13

****
I am the vine, ye are the branches: He that abideth in me, and I in him, the same bringeth forth much fruit: for without me ye can do nothing. Herein is my Father glorified, that ye bear much fruit; so shall ye be my disciples.

– John 5:15
****

Have you had the following experience I've had from time to time? If, as a result of the hustle and bustle of daily life, I am unable to read my Bible and pray regularly I begin to grow weak in my Christian walk.

Healthcare professionals and others working in professions and jobs requiring them to do overnight duty may bear me out—we usually return home from overnight sessions really exhausted. We may wake up from our rest only to realise there is not much time left for us to get ready for yet another gruesome overnight duty. Under such circumstances we may hardly find time for meaningful Bible study and prayer.

Of course, it is not only those in healthcare professions and others exposed to overnight duty who may undergo the type of experience outlined above.

It is important, Christian soldiers, when undergoing a spiritual low in our Christian walk that we read the alarm signals early in order to take steps to charge our spiritual batteries in good time, so we do not fall back, yes even backslide.

I pray the Lord to help us develop and maintain a healthy work/life balance, to prevent us from becoming burnt out, not only physically, but also spiritually.

March 14

****
Ho, every one that thirsteth, come ye to the waters, and he that hath no money; come ye, buy, and eat; yea, come, buy wine and milk without money and without price.

– Isaiah 55:1-3
****

I did not receive any pocket money from my parents; the same could be said of every child growing up in our community. When we were big enough to do so, my peers and I found avenues by which we could earn some money for ourselves.

One avenue by which we did so involved clearing cocoa farms of weeds prior to the cocoa harvest.

At other times we went about hunting animals such as squirrels, Gambian pouched rats, grass-cutters, etc. Sometimes we returned empty-handed. At other times luck smiled on us—we returned home with our hunting sack filled with various kinds of game. We gave part of our catch to our parents and sold the rest. The money we obtained was shared equally among ourselves.

Sometimes each of us contributed part of our earnings towards a feast. On such occasions we purchased rice and some provisions from the village shop and met at the home of one of us to cook and enjoy our meal. To avoid the situation where some of us might keep our monies and refuse to contribute anything only to turn up when the meal was ready to be served, appeal to our kindness and hope to be offered something to eat, we abided strictly by the rule: "No contribution, no chop!"—NCNC for short. (*Chop* was broken English for "to eat.")

Is it not comforting, fellow Christian soldiers, that unlike the rules by which my peers and I organised our coking events during my boyhood days in my little village, we do not have to contribute anything towards the Lord's feast? Indeed, not only is our salvation free, we also do not need to pay for our passage to the New Jerusalem. Indeed, so long as we hold on to our Living Lord, we are guaranteed a free passage!

March 15

****
Watch and pray, that ye enter not into temptation: the spirit indeed is willing, but the flesh is weak.

– Matthew 26:41
****

Christian friend battling with temptation,
I urge you not to allow the beautiful things of this world
to distract you from what really matters in this life–
a close walk with the Lord of Hosts.
The beauty of this world is like the flowers of the fields
that blossom today and tomorrow wither away.
Why then allow the temporal to draw you from that
which matters most–
eternal fellowship with the Prince of Princes and Lord of Lords?

Dear Christian soldier, what is becoming a stumbling block
between you and your walk with the Lord?
The beautiful ladies walking the streets?
The handsome and athletic young men
crossing your paths?
Oh, there are millions upon millions of them!
And every day that passes by,
Almighty Father by His grace allows
several thousands more to be added to the number.
Do not allow the lust of the flesh to draw you away from
the Good Shepherd.

I implore you rather to seek first the Kingdom of God
and His righteousness and
He will in His own right time provide for all your needs.

Dear child of God, is it the love of money
that impedes your journey to Calvary's mountain?
Money, the devil with many names and faces—the root
of all evils,
the source of conflict too numerous to list—among
married couples, parents and
children, brothers and sisters, nations and kingdoms?
Wealth indeed can win us many admirers.
Let our money take wings one day and fly away,
and we will in a twinkle of an eye lose our
numerous admirers!
So why allow that which is worldly and temporal—
silver, diamonds and gold
stand between you and your ever faithful Friend?
Materialism, the love of material goods—that is but
building on sand!
If there is any sure foundation to build on, it is the Rock
of Ages cleft for us.

March 16

****

> **Because I have called, and ye refused; I have stretched out my hand, and no man regarded; But ye have set at nought all my counsel, and would none of my reproof:**
>
> **I also will laugh at your calamity; I will mock when your fear cometh;**
>
> **When your fear cometh as desolation, and your destruction cometh as a whirlwind; when distress and anguish cometh upon you. Then shall they call upon me, but I will not answer; they shall seek me early, but they shall not find me: For that they hated knowledge, and did not choose the fear of the Lord: They would none of my counsel: they despised all my reproof.**
>
> **– Proverbs 1:24-30**

****

Have you sat down to consider the matter, my dear friend? Whenever there is a catastrophic event on our planet, be it natural or man-made, the world tends to ask the question: "If there is a God why did He allow such a heinous crime or catastrophic earthquake, tsunami, drought, etc., to happen?"

Is it not strange, my good friends, how the world seems to consider God as a kind of spare tyre that they consult only in times of emergency?

When they meet to party and enjoy their lives, who cares about God?

When the lovers of the game of football gather at a huge sports stadium in one of the world capitals and also around TV sets around the globe to enjoy the FIFA World Cup final, who in such moments think about Almighty God?

When the world gathers around their TV sets to enjoy the American Super Bowl, does anyone in such ecstatic moments thank Almighty God for the free oxygen at our disposal?

Come catastrophe and disaster, then the world begins all of a sudden to heap insults at the Ancient of Days! What a patient and big-hearted God He is! If indeed we happened to possess the power and authority at the disposal of the Rock of Ages, wouldn't we consider immediate retribution against such a bunch of insolents, known as humanity, who have the audacity to behave in such an appalling manner?

Dear Christian soldier, I pray the Lord to give us strength to endure whatever may come our way, however unpalatable it may be, and resist the temptation to question His love .

MARCH 17

****

Pharaoh said to Joseph, "See, I have set you over all the land of Egypt.

– Genesis 41:41

****

What thoughts might have gone through the mind of the prisoner Joseph as he retired to bed in the night prior to the day of his miraculous turn-around experience?

May I beg to conjecture: get up as usual, get a few dry pieces of bread for breakfast, bleak future, indefinite incarceration, no hope of ever meeting his family, no hope of marrying and producing a child, no hope, no hope…

What are the thoughts going through your mind today, my dear Christian? No hope of finding work; no hope of paying your rent, no hope of even earning enough for your upkeep? No hope of being able to bear your own children?

Please bear in mind that we serve a God who can turn us from Prisoners to Prime Ministers in the twinkle of an eye.

With that assurance in mind, just keep going; look up, and not down, until the "Turn Around!" God comes your way to turn your sorrow into joy, your affliction into delight, your poverty into prosperity.

MARCH 18

Is anything too hard for the LORD? At the time appointed I will return unto thee, according to the time of life, and Sarah shall have a son.

– Genesis 18:14

"Is anything too hard for the Lord?" The answer of course is a big NO!

Unfortunately, when confronted with difficulties, when after we have prayed, prayed and prayed; yes, when after we have fasted and fasted our problems are not going away, we have the tendency to waver, indeed to vacillate, yes, to falter.

There is a saying that: we must expect the worst while hoping for the best. As far as the believer is concerned, the WORST can NEVER be the end game. The seemingly worst scenario may seem to tarry long—longer than we might have anticipated, longer for our liking.

At the end of the day, however, if we hold on, the BEST will surely be ours, for indeed nothing is too difficult for the Lord who has called us to service.

MARCH 19

****

But Simon's wife's mother lay sick of a fever, and anon they tell him of her. And he came and took her by the hand, and lifted her up; and immediately the fever left her, and she ministered unto them.

– Mark 1:30 & 31

****

We are not told how long she had been in bed—a day, a couple of days, a week, perhaps? Also, apart from stating that she was in bed with fever, the Bible does not reveal any further details as to the cause of the disease. Still, we can deduce that, whatever the underlying cause of her condition, she was generally unwell at the time of the Lord's arrival.

It was at the very moment when the relatives were grappling with their helplessness in the face of the disease that Doctor Jesus, whose healing powers know no bounds, appeared on the scene. And he came and took her by the hand, and lifted her up; and immediately the fever left her, and she ministered unto them.

Yes, enter the Great Physician, and disease, whatever the cause, begins to shake, begins to tremble to its core. In this particular case, the Lord touched the afflicted woman. He did not need to do so though. As in various other instances, He just spoke the word and disease, whatever the cause, just took flight and vanished!

Dear Christian Soldier, whatever disease that may be afflicting you, your family or dear ones, I pray for Divine Intervention in Jesus Name!

MARCH 20

> **For the mountains shall depart, and the hills be removed; but my kindness shall not depart from thee, neither shall the covenant of my peace be removed, saith the Lord that hath mercy on thee.**
>
> *– Isaiah 54:10*

Assuring words, really assuring words! A promise of everlasting kindness! Mountains and hills rarely move; whereas earthquakes are able to cause small hills and hillocks to crumble, they are unlikely to impact on well-established mountains the likes of the Alps, Everest, Kilimanjaro, etc., however massive the force with which they strike.

The above verse declares that even should an earthquake cause a huge mountain to crumble, the love and kindness of the heavenly father will abide forever.

Child of God who may be undergoing severe mental agony; who is brooding over the misfortune that has visited your home, get up; I urge you to take comfort in the assuring words of our Heavenly Father. For sure, no matter how protracted the battle may turn out to be, be assured of Divine help, kindness and peace.

MARCH 21

****

Therefore we do not lose heart. Even though our outward man is perishing, yet the inward man is being renewed day by day.

– 2 Corinthians 4:10

****

I am not blowing my own trumpet before the whole world. The fact is, I consider myself generally hardworking. Mother and father were both hardworking, working hard from the rising of the sun till its setting to provide for their children. Did they pass on that trait to me? I have indeed been active throughout my life.

Of late though, I have begun to realise something—as much as I would like to perform just the way I did in my twenties, thirties, even my forties, my body is simply refusing to obey my commands. Even if it does, I realise at the end of the day, that my body requires more time than it did previously to recover.

The ageing process, no doubt, has slowly but surely come into play.

One thing which I find comforting in my situation, however, is the realisation that even though I am physically weakened with the years, spiritually that is not the case.

Although exposed each day to the vicissitudes of life, the Lord by His grace gives me the spiritual strength each day to cope with my situation. I do not know what tomorrow holds in store for me, but the assurance that the same Almighty God who was my protector yesterday, who has been protecting me today and will be standing guard by my bed as I retire to sleep tonight, will surely be with me on waking up tomorrow is very comforting, to put it mildly.

MARCH 22

****
And Jesus said unto the centurion, Go thy way; and as thou hast believed, so be it done unto thee. And his servant was healed in the selfsame hour.

– Matthew 8:13

****

Amazing, Amazing, Amazing! The Lord speaks and healing takes place!

Strictly speaking, the Divine does not heal, does not mend or repair damaged tissue or organs. Instead, the Divine creates—not gradually, but instantaneously. He does not for example repair or mend a diseased kidney or liver but rather creates a new one to replace the old one damaged by disease. As He says, "I make all things new." (Revelation 21:5.)

The Lord of Creation does not require surgical instruments to carry out surgical repair of a perforated appendix, a brain abscess, a liver cyst, a broken bone or whatever. He just creates new tissue or organs to replace the diseased or injured component.

The Lord of Creation does not need to mend broken bones. Without the shedding of blood, without pain to the patient, without the need to swallow painkillers to ease pain, the Divine executes His surgery to restore broken bones and diseased organs.

In the presence of the Divine, the functioning of organs does not merely improve, but regains ideal values. Blood sugar values are restored to normalcy in the diabetic, clotting values normalise in the haemophilic, sickle red blood cells are restored to normal shapes in the patient tormented by the severe form of sickle cell anaemia, and so forth.

What else do we expect? Indeed, what options do the organs and tissue have but to perform optimally in the presence of He who created them?

Are you or your loved ones afflicted with a seemingly incurable disease, just as in the case of my own son diagnosed with autism?

Let us join hands in prayer for their restoration. Yes, please remember me in your prayers just as I pray for you.

May the Great Physician of all times visit our homes at His own appointed time and bring a change—not to our glory but to the glory of His Mighty Name.

MARCH 23

****

And rend your heart, and not your garments, and turn unto the LORD your God: for he is gracious and merciful, slow to anger, and of great kindness, and repenteth him of the evil.

– Joel 2:13

****

As I worked in prison as a prison doctor, a young man of about 20 came to prison and I engaged him in conversation. The reason for his incarceration, he told me, was that he had disobeyed a court injunction order not to approach the residence of his mother. He confessed that he was indeed a troubled person who was causing his mother with whom he lived alone a "hell of a lot of problems".

Initially he abided by the court order. Soon, however, he began to yearn for his mother. No longer able to bear being away from her, he broke the injunction and approached her. Her mother on her part, unable to bear his presence, informed the police who came for him.

What a tragic story. I have not ceased from praying for them, that they would find a more amicable solution to their family problem.

Let us thank God that He has a big heart for the sinner, His wayward children; indeed, no matter how far away we wander astray, if we repent and return, He will accept us back into His fold.

MARCH 24

****

> Five times I received from the Jews the forty lashes minus one.
>
> Three times I was beaten with rods, once I was pelted with stones, three times I was shipwrecked, I spent a night and a day in the open sea,
>
> I have been constantly on the move. I have been in danger from rivers, in danger from bandits, in danger from my fellow Jews, in danger from Gentiles; in danger in the city, in danger in the country, in danger at sea; and in danger from false believers.
>
> I have laboured and toiled and have often gone without sleep; I have known hunger and thirst and have often gone without food; I have been cold and naked.
>
> Besides everything else, I face daily the pressure of my concern for all the churches. Who is weak, and I do not feel weak? Who is led into sin, and I do not inwardly burn?
>
> – 2 Corinthians 11:24-29

****

Dear Christian soldiers, I want us to ponder over the above scripture as we go about our daily activities on the battlefield of life. I am not advocating that trouble comes our way. We must indeed be happy if our day goes smoothly, devoid of troubles.

If on the other hand we are confronted with troubles, we should bear in mind that afflictions are not unique to us. Instead of moaning, yes instead of engaging in endless self-pity, we should instead pray the Lord to give us the grace to endure, for just as sure as the African sun will appear in the skies the next day (it usually does even after a day of persistent rainfall), in the same way, Heaven is sure to visit our home to put a smile on our faces. So, get up and start jumping for Jesus!

MARCH 25

****

But they that wait upon the LORD **shall renew their strength; they shall mount up with wings as eagles; they shall run, and not be weary; and they shall walk, and not faint.**

– Isaiah 40:31

****

Several years ago, I was an Asylum seeker in West Germany threatened with deportation. I was really distressed; I found no way out of my seemingly hopeless situation.

The Lord in His mercy led me to a church which was attended mainly by the American military community there. There was a Gospel concert going on. The moment I entered the hall and took my seat, the pastor got up to introduce the next song.

"Friend," he declared, "when you come to the end of your rope, you just don't give up. Rather tie a knot at the end and wait for the Lord to come your way. Be assured of this – He will surely come.'

The words penetrated deep into my heart. I felt God speaking to me through His servant. Though my problems did not dissipate immediately, the words gave me succour and support in time of great need. In the end I was spared deportation at the very last minute. Having been granted a student's visa, I was able to begin my studies at the Hanover Medical School.

Does it appear as if you have come to the end of your road? Are you stranded in the arid desert of your life, with no shelter around to shield you from the scorching sun, and you are sweating, sweating, sweating? You are threatened with a slow and agonizing death – dehydration, multiple organ failure and finally cardiac arrest? You look all around you, and help seems nowhere near. The countdown to your certain demise is slowly but surely heading towards zero. Even in such a dire situation, I urge you, child of God, not to give up, but rather to tie a knot and wait for the appearance of the turnaround God. He is not known to desert His own. Yes, for sure, come your way He surely will.

March 26

Beloved, I wish above all things that thou mayest prosper and be in health, even as thy soul prospereth.

– 3 John 2

Good health—how precious it is, my fellow Christian friends.

Indeed, when I sit down to consider, yes ponder over all the possible factors, causes, incidents, that could apply to one, who wakes up healthy and strong only to die on a particular day!

Indeed, if we consider that anything could happen to us at a particular moment to deprive our brain of its oxygen supply over a period of about five minutes, a situation that could lead to irreparable brain damage and our deaths, we would be singing from morning till evening about the goodness of the Lord, instead of murmuring about trivial matters.

Please permit me to list a few of the countless unexpected events that could occur without warning, that may pre-empt the state of affairs alluded to above: choking (caused perhaps by a chunk of food); heart attack; stroke; pulmonary embolism; anaphylactic shock, severe bleeding; a stray bullet, a gas explosion, a car crash—the list is endless.

If in spite of all these possible causes of death on a particular day, the Lord has increased our stay on earth by even a day, you and I should be grateful to our Maker, instead of brooding and murmuring over this and that!

March 27

****

The fool hath said in his heart, There is no God. They are corrupt, they have done abominable works, there is none that doeth good.

The Lord looked down from heaven upon the children of men, to see if there were any that did understand, and seek God.

– Psalm 14:1-2

****

Be warned, child of God, of the so-called masters of knowledge who walk the surface of the earth: academics, experts, highly-learned, they enjoy the acclaim of the world; imbued with the spirit of secularism, they go about spreading their ideas. They are held in high-esteem by an adoring society; whatever issues out of their mouths is regarded by their teeming followers as ultimate truth.

Resist the temptation, child of God, resist the temptation to swim with the tide of time! Do not lose sight of one thing: mere mortals they are, these heroes of society. They are equipped like you and me with brain cells limited by the Almighty in dimensions! Can a brain of flesh comprehend the deep, deep secrets that belong only to the Creator God Himself? So, beware, child of God! Do not be swayed by strutting men from the Holy Truths laid out in the Word of God! Instead, I entreat you to trust in the One and only Source of wisdom, the Lord Almighty, Maker of Heaven and Earth: All that is seen and unseen—YAHWEH, who is all-seeing and all-powerful!

MARCH 28

****
Because thou hast made the LORD**, which is my refuge, even the most High, thy habitation; there shall no evil befall thee, neither shall any plague come nigh thy dwelling.**

– Psalm 91:9- 10
****

One day in November, 2018, as I listened to the radio while driving to a meeting, it was reported that the database of a renowned international hotel had been compromised, leading to the data of millions of their customers being stolen.

That led me to reflect on matters related to the spiritual realm of our existence. Every day Satan is going around, stealing and compromising the database of human beings and thereby enslaving them.

Christian soldiers need not fear the foe, however. For, because we have made the LORD our refuge, "no evil shall befall us; neither shall any plague come nigh our dwelling."

Yes indeed, the Lord we serve has built a super virus defence system around us so we do not need to fear the clandestine attempts of the Devil to infiltrate our spiritual computer, our divine software, to damage our system and take control over us.

March 29

***

Then he said unto them, Go your way, eat the fat, and drink the sweet, and send portions unto them for whom nothing is prepared: for this day is holy unto our Lord: neither be ye sorry; for the joy of the Lord is your strength.

– Nehemiah 8:10

***

I first came in contact with my German pastor friend, Gottfried—bless him—in October 1984. Shortly prior to our meeting he and his family had returned from a trip to Cameroon. They were there to visit a family friend, a citizen of the West African country who had returned to his country after completing his medical studies in Germany.

"I enjoyed my stay in Africa," he told me. "I was pleasantly surprised to notice the smile, the joy on the faces of the people I met on the streets, individuals who though materially poorer than my fellow citizens in Germany, appeared, no doubt, to be happier than my countrymen I meet on our streets."

Whereas we must do all in our power to reduce material poverty if not completely eliminate it, the fact still remains that pure happiness is not obtained through material wealth.

It is indeed true, my fellow Christian friend, that the joy of the Lord is our strength and not the things of this world.

MARCH 30

And when they came to Marah, they could not drink of the waters of Marah, for they were bitter: therefore the name of it was called Marah.

– Exodus 15:23

Dear Christian friend, at this hour as you are reading through these lines, you, like the children of Israel on their way to the promised land, may be standing by your well of Marah. Sweating and thirsty as you journey to the New Jerusalem, you have spotted a fountain of water in the arid land you are journeying through. Hoping to quench your thirst, you have hurried to it. With the help of your folded palm you gulp the seemingly fresh water down your throat. Next moment you spit everything out of your mouth! Bitter as gall, bitter as gall! Your only hope of quenching your thirst has turned out to be as bitter as gall! Furious, you are about to curse God and die!

Be strong and courageous, child of God, for that is not the end of your story. Surely, your destiny will not be sealed at Marah! No, never! Yes, indeed, instead of giving up, I urge you to go on your knees in prayer and implore Almighty God to intervene to turn your situation around.

Surely, in His own right time, I AM WHO I AM will come your way to turn your sorrow into joy. So hold on, yes stand firm and don't quit, my fellow Christian soldier!

MARCH 31

****

And they came to Elim, where were twelve wells of water, and threescore and ten palm trees: and they encamped there by the waters.

– Exodus 15:27

****

Yesterday the bitter waters of Marah, today the sweet waters of Elim. We do, indeed serve a turnaround God. Though He may seem to delay, yes He may seem to tarry too long for our liking, in his own time, He surely will come our way.

Dear Christian friend, have your debts piled up into a heap, as tall as Mount Everest? Have your bills risen to high heaven? And try as you may, your business just won't take off? Not that you are someone who can be described as lazy. On the contrary, you are a born workaholic. You have poured your resources, your strength, your energy into your enterprise, yet your business just won't pick up! Not that you failed to research the market before establishing your company. On the contrary, you took pains to do a thorough market research. Indeed, all the experts you contacted gave you a good chance of success. Undoubtedly you have done all that is humanly possible to ensure the success of your enterprise, yet still the business just won't flourish. The bills, in the meantime, are piling up, piling up, piling up. The clock is ticking towards midnight, towards the dawn of the day when your creditors have threatened legal action to reclaim their money. You cannot imagine any way of escape. Still, I urge you not to give up! No matter the problems facing you, child of God, I urge you to look beyond the circumstances – soon, very soon, you will reach the sweet waters of Elim.

APRIL 1

****
But if ye will not do so, behold, ye have sinned against the LORD: and be sure your sin will find you out.
– Numbers 32:23
****

If the Word of God admonishes us to live holy lives and flee from the lusts of the flesh and other deeds unbecoming of our holy calling, we seem to think that our Heavenly father is being too bossy, placing one restriction after the other on us.

If we are to sit down to ponder things over, we shall come to the conclusion that, at the end of the day, it is in our interest to heed the advice, for at the end of the day it us ourselves, not the Great High God, who benefits from keeping the rules. Well, we may decide to disobey, but then, as today's scripture warns us, our sins will come back to find us out.

In my work as a prison doctor I have come across several instances when "the sins of others have found them out." To save time, I will limit myself to only one example.

It involved a gentleman who was sentenced for a rape charge. This, according to his account, was how things unfolded. He began cheating on his wife. A time came when his mistress asked him to raise a substantial loan so they could purchase a house. He refused. That led the mistress to hatch a story – accusing him of rape. As the police went about investigating the case, they went to his marital home to do a search. It was then that his shell-shocked wife learnt about his double life.

In the end he was sentenced for rape. Things did not end there – his wife divorced him and restricted his access to their two young children. At the time I met him his world had fallen apart. He told me he wished the clock of time could be turned back to the time when he had not met his mistress. "Given a second chance, I would turn away and run away from her, as far as my legs could carry me!" he stressed.

Dear Fellow soldier, we need indeed to draw close to the Lord, so we won't fall short of our holy calling and eventually get ourselves into trouble.

APRIL 2

****
Ye are the salt of the earth: but if the salt have lost his savour, wherewith shall it be salted? it is thenceforth good for nothing, but to be cast out, and to be trodden under foot of men.

– Matthew 5:13-16
****

One of my close associates at medical school was an Iranian citizen.

Because both of us lived in the same hostel, and also because both of us frequented the library situated not far from our hostel, our ways crossed on an almost daily basis. As in the case of the great majority of Iranians, he was of the Islamic faith – a mainstream Moslem; not by any means a radical.

Occasionally we engaged in conversation, not arguments, centred around our respective faiths. Like other Moslems, he held the view that Jesus was not the Son of God but, like Mohammed, one of the prophets.

One day he saw me riding a brand-new bike presented to me by a Christian friend.

"Where did you get that from?"

"It is a gift from a Christian friend." was my reply.

"Was that individual willing to part with such an amazing sports bike without demanding any money in return?"

"Yes indeed," I responded.

Not long after the above conversation, I showed him a well sought-after anatomy book presented to me as a gift by my pastor friend.

"You got that also for free?" he inquired, the surprise written clearly on his face

"Yes indeed!"

A short while later I showed him a letter from a German foundation granting me a scholarship for the remaining term of my studies.

"Hey Robert, come on, your Jesus is really generous to you! He is indeed showering you with one gift after the other!"

"Come and taste His goodness!" I replied. "He will not only shower you with material gifts but He will grant you eternal life!"

"No, no, I am convinced of my faith – nothing will change that!" he replied

I have not ceased from praying for him. Though I have in the meantime missed his contact, I continue to remember him in my prayers, that the Lord will open his eyes, that he may see.

Dear Fellow Christian soldier, let us through our deeds and words, be an example to the lost world, that many may come to glorify the Lord or Redeemer.

APRIL 3

****
The horse is made ready for the day of battle, but victory rests with the LORD**.**

– **Proverbs 21:31 (NIV)**
****

Claim your victory in the Mighty Name of God;
victory over all the forces that seek to pull you down –
the forces of darkness, the host of the forces of evil that walk in darkness
like roaring lions seeking someone to devour.
No, child of the Living God, do not be overcome by the intimidations of Satan!
So affirm your victory over all the forces tormenting you!

Claim you victory over poverty, want and disease,
Problems that seeks to pin you down,
Do not despair, soldier of Christ,
instead I urge you to assert your victory over
the difficulties in the Name of the Morning Star!

Claim your victory, child of God,
over bitterness and an unforgiving spirit,
over gossiping and backbiting,
over the spirit of vengeance and retaliation,
over the spirit of pride and self-esteem,
over hatred and enmity,
over love of power and money,
over all the other negative influences,
that bring the Name of the Lord our Righteousness into disrepute.
So claim your victory in the Holy Blood of Jesus!

APRIL 4

****

Jesus saith unto him, I am the way, the truth, and the life: no man cometh unto the Father, but by me.

– John 14:6

****

As I left home one day to travel for a meeting in London, apart from the address I had in hand, I had no idea at all of the place I was heading for – it was the first time I was travelling to that location. How do I get there? Well, I fed the address into my satellite navigation system – SAT NAV – and set out on my journey.

"Turn right; turn left; go straight on...," the device kept on instructing me – or was it commanding me! In the end it got me to my destination.

The satellite navigation system – what a wonderful invention of the human brain! As in all human inventions, it has its flaws. There have been cases when the Sat Nav has directed its users to the wrong places. Generally speaking though, it accomplishes what it is required to do – to lead to the destinations it is programmed to do.

Dear Christian Friends, we have a more perfect, yes, a more sure SAT NAV, a GPS system that ERRS NOT – the Holy Spirit of the Living Lord sent to guide and lead us to the New Jerusalem. Let us obediently follow Him in all that we do, and He will surely lead us to our destination.

Yes indeed, our Loving Lord is *the way, the truth, and the life* to our loving Father.

APRIL 5

****
For God has not given us a spirit of fear, but of power and of love and of a sound mind.

– 2 Timothy 1:7
****

Fear (English); kǒngjù (Chinese); peur (French); angst (German); temor (Spanish); ehuu (Twi) – you are free to supplement the list with your own vernacular for the word *fear*!

We have the tendency to harbour all kinds of fear. Time and space will not permit me to list all the types of fear we are plagued with. I cite only three examples here—

*Some of us have a family history of this-and-that type of cancer and are tormented with the fear of developing them ourselves.

*Some of us have invested our money in stocks and live in constant fear of losing all or part of our investments through a crash on the stock exchange market.

*Some of us are foreigners living either illegally or living with temporarily visas in a foreign country and live in constant fear of being deported back to their native countries to face an uncertain future.

For sure, being Soldiers of the cross, does not make us immune from exposure to the various vicissitudes of this world. Whatever the nature of the uncertain situation we are exposed to however, let us learn to bring them before the Lord in prayer and not be scared by them, for truly "For God has not given us a spirit of fear, but of power and of love and of a sound mind."

April 6

****

Why do the nations conspire and the peoples plot in vain? The kings of the earth rise up and the rulers band together against the Lord and against his anointed, saying, "Let us break their chains and throw off their shackles.

– Psalm 2:1-3

****

Let us imagine that the whole of Mankind, divided as we are today into nations, tribes, national, political, economic, social, religious blocks, should for a moment join our military capabilities together in a conflict against the Army of Almighty God! Yes, let the whole of Mankind gather together all the military arsenals at its disposal – the immense military might of NATO, spearheaded by the USA, plus that of Russia, China, Israel, India, Brazil, Argentina, South Africa, Ghana, Nigeria, etc. Yes, let us gather together an Army Universum, equipped with weapons boasting the latest technology of the 21st century – satellite-guided intercontinental ballistic missiles, bunker breaking missiles, panzer-breaking assault missiles (you can go on listing them until the cows come home) and pitch ourselves in a battle against the Army of the Holy One. Yes, imagine that – the totality of Army Mankind Rebellious against the forces of the Creator God! Awesome, awesome! And yet what does such a power amount to, all the forces of Army Mankind Rebellious, when pitted against the authority of the Lord Zebaoth? Nuclear Weapons? Forget! Chemical Weapons? Peanuts! Biological Warfare? Who created the germs to begin with?

My dear Christian friend, is it not a shame that we have the tendency to project the enemy as huge, yes as gigantic, gargantuan, mammoth, etc., instead of focusing on the fact that "greater is He that is in us than he that is in the world"? (1 John 4:4)

Come on, fellow Soldiers of the Cross, let us brush aside the fears and apprehensions that plague us and let us move forward with all boldness on our journey to the Promised Land.

April 7

***

For I know the plans I have for you," declares the Lord, "plans to prosper you and not to harm you, plans to give you hope and a future.

– Jeremiah 29:11 (NIV)

***

Some people are by nature pessimists; they see the bottle always as half empty; such individuals have the tendency to grumble all the time.

Others are by nature optimists who see the bottle as half full all the time. Even before becoming a Christian, I could be counted with the born optimists.

Christians by our call should be optimists; we should see the bottle as half full always, because unlike other members of our race, we serve a Master who knows the end from the beginning.

Indeed, we fight in a battalion which knows no defeat!

Accra Hearts of Oak, one of the well-established football teams in my native Ghana, has as their motto: "Never say die until the bones are rotten!"

Christian soldiers on the battlefield of life might as well make that motto their own. We should indeed never say die until the bones are rotten – for indeed if we are to fall on the battlefield, we shall be with the Lord, 'ere our bones are rotten!!

APRIL 8

****
Jesus answered and said unto him, Art thou a master of Israel, and knowest not these things?

– John 3:10
****

Professor Dr Nicodemus – what a learned fellow he was; well versed in the things of this world but almost ignorant in spiritual matters.

There are indeed millions of his kind walking the surface of the earth, very well-versed in academics, holding academic titles from renowned Universities stretching from North to South, East and West! Nothing wrong with academic titles, more grease on your laurels – your hard work should be honoured; nevertheless, Master Jesus has these questions for such title bearers:

"Are you the Professor of Anatomy, yes, are you a person who derives your living by teaching the parts of the human body I created and you still don't believe that I created the human body? Are you so versed in the intricacies of the human body I created and still don't get it – that the body you are working with, yes, that the human body you are working with is too complex to have come about out of mere chance?"

"Are you highly regarded, Professor of Physics, and do not accept that the laws of Physics could not have developed out of sheer accident?"

"Are you professor of Theology and you don't get this – that the bottom line is that in reality, no one can study ME—yes that my workings are too mysterious for anyone to comprehend?"

"Do you bear the title of Bishop or Archbishop and yet do not grasp that the bottom line is that I do not dwell in church buildings but in hearts?"

Fellow Christian Soldiers, may we always bear in mind that we indeed serve Almighty God who is omnipotent and omnipresent, yes who is a spirit who accompanies us wherever the sun dawns on us, that we strive to live lives worthy of our Christian calling, not now and then – but all the time.

APRIL 9

****
Be careful for nothing; but in everything by prayer and supplication with thanksgiving let your requests be made known unto God. And the peace of God, which passeth all understanding, shall keep your hearts and minds through Christ Jesus.

– Philippians 4:6-7
****

Anxiety can be a terrible thing. Anxious thoughts, much as they are terrible during the day, are even more dreadful at night. They can, among others rob, us of sleep, sleep that is meant to make us feel refreshed for the next day.

Lack of sleep on its part leads to a feeling of tiredness during the day.

If one is alone at home and does not have to go to work, lack of sleep during the night could force us to sleep during the day, to make up for the lost sleep at night. Such a situation could lead to a disturbed sleep pattern for once we sleep heavily during the day, we may find it difficult to sleep at night, so a vicious circle is the result.

For those who have to go to work after a sleepless night, the disturbed sleep could lead to lack of concentration, even irritability at the work place.

The disturbed sleep may eventually lead us to consult our doctor for sleeping pills, which taken for the short term might restore the sleep pattern. We may however come to rely on the medication for the long term, which could lead to addiction.

We are called upon not to be anxious for nothing. Accepted, it is not always easy to overcome our anxieties. As Christian soldiers we can resort to reading the word of God and prayers to help us overcome our anxious moments. I personally experienced much help in prayer and fasting to overcome periods of extreme distress in my Christian walk. Indeed, prayer combined with fasting could constitute a useful strategy to help us deal with anxious moments along our Christian journey.

I pray the Good Lord to refresh and energize Christian soldiers experiencing despairing moments in their Christian walk, today and forever, Amen.

APRIL 10

****

Flee also youthful lusts: but follow righteousness, faith, charity, peace, with them that call on the Lord out of a pure heart

– 2 Timothy 2:22

****

At the time I was growing up, one of the scenarios I dreaded most was a confrontation with a snake. Indeed, the danger was real. Contrary to the situation of my peers who lived in areas of the world devoid of snakes, we who lived at Mpintimpi were in real danger of being bitten by them. So, whenever we went to work on the farm I was always on the watch for the dreadful crawling reptiles of creation.

When I eventually came across one, I took to my heels at the fastest of speeds, never mind if the distance between human and reptile was considerable. I did not wait to categorize the danger. As far as I was concerned, so long as the danger was within visual (seeing) distance, it was enough reason for me to run for my life.

Flee from youthful lusts, Apostle Paul is pleading with Timothy. Mobilize all your strength and energy fellow Christian soldier and take to your heels when confronted with youthful lusts, the senior ranking officer in the Army of Christ implores his junior.

During my time working as a General Practitioner (family doctor) in Germany, one of my patients who had just returned from a short stay in our native Ghana entered my consultation room one day and began:

"Doc, please test me for HIV! I am really scared I might have contracted the virus. I had a one-off adventure with a lady to whom I offered a lift. Now since my return I have noticed some spots on my body. I am also feeling generally unwell. I am really scared; I am experiencing sleepless nights!"

The test was done as requested – it came back negative. I asked him to return after a while for a second test. The second test confirmed the previous one.

"Thank God, everything is okay; the last several weeks have been a nightmare!" he stated.

To please our Commander-in-Chief in particular, and also to be spared sleepless nights, diseases, pain, broken relations, etc., we better heed Apostle Paul's advice and take to our heels when confronted with "youthful lusts" of any kind.

April 11

****

Take therefore no thought for the morrow: for the morrow shall take thought for the things of itself. Sufficient unto the day the evil thereof.

– Matthew 6:34

****

Today is a unique day the Lord has made. Let us be glad and rejoice in it. Yesterday is gone and will never come back. Tomorrow may never come; so we have TODAY to enjoy. Whatever the problems facing us, let us gather strength of spirit to face them. Indeed, whatever problems befall us today, let us look them in the face and declare with boldness:

We are Christian Soldiers;

we fight on the side of a triumphant army;

though the battle might seem to be going against us,

victory is assured in Jesus' Name.

Stay blessed, fellow soldier of the cross of Calvary!

April 12

****
The Lord trieth the righteous: but the wicked and him that loveth violence his soul hateth.

– Psalm 11:5
****

Harry Smith , a fellow soldier of the Cross of Calvary, had this to say concerning the first part of Psalm 11:5 – *the Lord trieth the righteous...*

"Since we are not in paradise, but in the wilderness, we must look for one trouble after another. As a bear came to David after a lion, and a giant after a bear, and a king after a giant, and Philistines after a king, so, when believers have fought with poverty, they shall fight with envy; when they have fought with envy, they shall fight with infamy; when they have fought with infamy, they shall fight with sickness; they shall be like a labourer who is never out of work."

I pray Divine favour to accompany you, my fellow Christian warrior, throughout the day.

APRIL 13

****
There hath no temptation taken you but such as is common to man: but God is faithful, who will not suffer you to be tempted above that ye are able; but will with the temptation also make a way to escape, that ye may be able to bear it.
– 1 Corinthians 10:13
****

The first-year student at the university is not called upon to write the papers meant for the final year.

A junior doctor aspiring to become a surgeon who has only a few weeks of training behind him/her is not called upon to perform complicated heart surgery.

Abraham was not asked to sacrifice Isaac in the first year of his studies in the Divine University of Trials and Afflictions.

When I was growing up in my little village, I and my six other siblings had to help our parents on the farm. Not only did we perform duties such as planting and harvesting crops such cocoa, maize, yams; we also helped by carrying on our heads items harvested on the farm on a particular day.

Our parents assigned us the loads based on our respective age and physical fitness. Our youngest sister, Afia for example, was not made to carry the load someone like myself, ten years her senior, was expected to be capable of carrying. It came down in the end to "everyone according to his or her ability."

Dear Christian friend battling with troubles, difficulties, yes, who might be tempted to sink in self pity as a result of the obstacles and impediments, I do sympathize with you. But the good news is that our Lord has promised us that we will not be allowed to be tempted beyond what we can bear. He will, in His own time, definitely come your way to end your troubles. Indeed, soon, very soon, your trials and afflictions, the challenges threatening to break your neck, will be over; so gather strength of spirit to carry on the fight.

April 14

****

God is our refuge and strength, a very present help in trouble. Therefore will not we fear, though the earth be removed, and though the mountains be carried into the midst of the sea.

– Psalm 46:1-2

****

The Psalmist declares among other things that Almighty God is *a present help in trouble*. It implies among other things that even though Satan and a host of demons surround us to aim countless sharp-pointed swords at our hearts, angels of Almighty God, under the control of our Divine Shepherd, will be at hand to ward off the malicious onslaught.

With that in mind, dear Fellow soldier of the Cross of Calvary, let's us face this day with the comfort, the assurance that no matter the obstacles the Enemy might place in our way, victory will be ours..

Stay blessed my dear Christian friends.

APRIL 15

****

Be strong, and let your heart take courage, all you who wait for the Lord!

– Psalm 31:24

****

In the Name of the Father
and of the Son and of the Holy Spirit,
Child of God being tormented by the devil,
I urge you not to give up the fight!
The battle indeed is fierce!
I see you bleeding from your wounds and gasping for air;
persevere, persevere, persevere to the end!
Yes indeed, it's just a matter of time when the tide will turn in your favour,
when victory, sweet victory, will smile on you.

In the Name of the Father
and of the Son and of the Holy Spirit,
child of God being given a good beating
by the principalities, the powers and
the rulers of the darkness of this world
inhabiting the high places,
I urge you to hold on to the painful end!
It is just a matter of time, I assure you,
when the Lord of Hosts will
dispatch His angels to your rescue!
Enough is enough! Leave my child in peace –
the Tormentor will be rebuked!
So gather strength and do not become resigned to your fate:
Soon, very soon, victory will be yours!

April 16

****
Know ye not that they which run in a race run all, but one receiveth the prize? So run, that ye may obtain.

– 1 Corinthians 9:24
****

I read about the feat of the late John Stephen Akhwari, a marathon runner who ran for his country, Tanzania, in the 1968 Mexico City Olympic Games. It was the last event of the games. Early in the race he suffered a bad fall and, in the process, badly injured his leg. Though he trailed a considerable distance behind the others, he kept running instead of giving up. In the end he finished the race nearly an hour behind the rest of the runners.

When Akhwari finally approached the stadium, running on his badly injured and hurting leg, it was nearly empty. As he entered the stadium the meagre crowd still present rose to their feet and began to cheer. Photographers scrambled to set up the cameras they had long since dismantled to capture what without doubt would be regarded as one of the greatest finishes in Olympics history. Later, when asked why he did not quit, Akhwari said simply: "My country did not send me 5,000 miles to start the race; they sent me 5,000 miles to finish the race!"

Come on, fellow Christian soldier considering to throw in the towel in the face of the hardships and difficulties confronting you. We did not enlist in the army of the Living Jesus only to surrender in the middle of the ferocious battle of life. No, never! We fight on the side of a winning army so victory is assured. So let's gather strength of spirit and keep on fighting in Jesus' Name!

April 17

****

Cast thy burden upon the Lord, and he shall sustain thee: he shall never suffer the righteous to be moved.

– Psalm 55:22

****

When I was growing up in the little village Mpintimpi, in Ghana, I assisted my parents in their daily chores, including work on the farm.

After several hours of hard work, we had to carry the crops harvested from the farmland on our heads over a considerable distance back home. Carrying the load on our heads was a neck-breaking affair. Our situation was not made easy by the scorching African sun. On other occasions, we were pounded mercilessly by torrential rains accompanied by ferocious winds.

Imagine, your neck breaking under the heavy load you are carrying and at the same time sweating under the scorching African sun, or being pounded mercilessly by torrential tropical rain! In such situations, the picture that would flash through my mind on a regular basis was the compound of our home. Nothing around me was important but home – home that would bring relief to my misery.

Dear Christian friend, whose neck is breaking under the heavy load you are bearing, I urge you to endure, yes to hold on, to keep focussed on your goal, on the Lord hanging on the cross of Calvary, bleeding and sweating, just for your sake! Soon, very soon, the Great Burden Bearer will come your way to relieve you of the load weighing you down.

So hold on, stand firm and don't quit!

APRIL 18

****
*And one of them smote the servant of the high priest, and cut off his right ear. And Jesus answered and said, Suffer ye thus far. And he touched his ear, and healed him.

– Luke 22:50-51

*Then Simon Peter having a sword drew it, and smote the high priest's servant, and cut off his right ear. The servant's name was Malchus. Then said Jesus unto Peter, Put up thy sword into the sheath: the cup which my Father hath given me, shall I not drink it?

– John 18:10-11
****

In considering the circumstances surrounding the incident, the heart of sinful man is apt to shout: "Hooray! It serves you right! You came to arrest and torture Peter's Master. You wanted to get at his Master—now Peter has got at you! That has nothing to do with an eye for an eye; no, it is purely a matter of self-defiance—nothing wrong with that!"

The onlookers, perhaps even those there to arrest Him, had probably expected the Lord to applaud Peter for fighting on His side, or at least to remain neutral and concentrate on issues relating to the appropriate strategy for saving His own skin. Instead, to the utter amazement of those present, He picks up the ear and replaces it—the wound instantly healed. Goodwill towards your enemy when he or she aims at your heart: absolutely incredible!

The Lord implores us to pray not only for those who like us, but also for our enemies! That is a tough call, a really tough call. May the Lord give us the needed grace to behave accordingly.

April 19

****

And when they were come to the place, which is called Calvary, there they crucified him, and the malefactors, one on the right hand, and the other on the left.

– Luke 23:33

****

How often do you and I moan, murmur, howl, whine over this and that. Sometimes I have the impression the human being was created to moan, howl, murmur from the rising of the sun right down to its setting.

Before I moved from my little impoverished village in Ghana to the wealthy West, I thought in view of the riches there, everyone would be happy—you may call it the simplified world outlook of a young teenager from rural Ghana! Well, I soon realized to my amazement that residents in the wealthy countries were also not free from moaning!

One would expect that Christians, because we serve Almighty God who knows the end from the beginning, to be less inclined to whinge. Well, I dare say that is not the case.

I am not implying I am an exemption to the case. One moment I am praising the Lord for helping me, despite seemingly insurmountable circumstances to make it to medical school in Hanover, Germany; the next moment I am cross with the Lord for not preventing my son from developing the condition of autism! Moaning yesterday, howling today, whining evermore!

Dear fellow soldiers of the Cross, whenever we are tempted to moan about our situation, indeed whine about our predicament, let us pause a moment and ask ourselves: have we been forced to carry a heavy cross along the streets to Jerusalem, to be nailed on the cross, indeed to be made to die a shameful death?

The fact is, even though we are not spared trouble for choosing to follow the Lord, we must keep in mind that we have not been made to bear a shameful cross and face a torturous death on the cross.

Dear Christina friends, whatever burdens we are bearing, let us pray for the needed grace to help us through. We have been promised by Scripture that we will not be tempted beyond what we are capable of bearing. The Lord indeed is faithful who will do just that.

APRIL 20

****

Jesus, when he had cried again with a loud voice, yielded up the ghost. And, behold, the veil of the temple was rent in twain from the top to the bottom; and the earth did quake, and the rocks rent; And the graves were opened; and many bodies of the saints which slept arose and came out of the graves after his resurrection, and went into the holy city, and appeared unto many.

– Matthew 27:50-53

****

Extraordinary, stunning, stupendous, phenomenal... words alone cannot describe the matter... are there any leading scholars of the English language that can help with further adjectives to describe what happened on that unique, indeed unrepeatable moment in Human history? In response to my appeal I hear someone at the other end of my street shouting out the words: awesome, miraculous, fantastic! Thanks for your help, dear friend, much appreciated!

As much as the adjectives above attempt to paint a picture of the extraordinary happenings on the outskirt of Jerusalem on the first Good Friday, a little over 2000 years ago, it is obvious they are insufficient, yes inadequate, to describe even in the minutest extent the events that unfolded on earth immediately after the Prince of Peace laid down his life, albeit temporally, on the cross of Calvary.

The veil of the temple, having lost its significance in Almighty God's plan of salvation, was torn into two by an invisible hand.

As if that were not enough, not only planet earth, but the whole universe began to quake, yes tremble, to shake uncontrollably in stunning respect for He who was and is and ever more shall be!

Even more astonishing, the graves of the righteous dead were no longer able to keep them, as they resurrected from the dead!

I often begin to shake my head in disbelief, yes in dismay when I read about ordinary men and women trying to explain the genesis of life, yes trying to put forward theories to explain not only the mystery of life but how the universe came onto existence.

Instead of keeping their mouths shut and admitting that such matters are beyond their ability to comprehend, they try to explain things away with their own brains, yes the human brain, which up till now is not even a hundred percent sure how itself functions!

Imagine that—the brain which cannot understand itself, going about trying to explain matters related to the workings of the Almighty!

Dear Christian soldier, we do indeed serve an awesome God, so keep your heads high and do not allow any problems, however huge, to cause you to abandon your hope in Christ the Resurrected one!

April 21

****

And as they were afraid, and bowed down their faces to the earth, they said unto them, Why seek ye the living among the dead? He is not here, but is risen: remember how he spake unto you when he was yet in Galilee, Saying, The Son of man must be delivered into the hands of sinful men, and be crucified, and the third day rise again.

– **Luke 24:5-7**

****

Christ is risen, Praise the Lord, Alleluia!

At the death of the Lord Jesus Christ his enemies thought that was the end of Him. Although during His life they had witnessed Him perform one amazing miracle after the other, including the raising of the dead, they thought the grave would be the end for Him, indeed that He would be confined to the grave till the end of time!

Indeed, just at the moment when His enemies were rejoicing over what they thought was His defeat at the hands of the Angel of Death, something beyond the ordinary happened—the Lord himself was resurrected from the dead!

Dear Christian soldier, our Lord is Risen from the dead indeed! That is our faith, that is our hope—not faith built on sand, not hope ungrounded, not fantasy, not delusion. Our faith is indeed hope built on solid foundations.

Certainly, our hope is grounded on a Rock, on the Prince of Peace, on the Divine Shepherd, on He who has the keys to the gates of hell and heaven.

So, let us, my fellow Christian soldiers, go into the world, yes the deep dark world of evil and proclaim the message of Hope. Yes, let us, with all energy and enthusiasm unceasingly broadcast the eternally assuring words of the True Shepherd:

I am he that liveth, and was dead; and, behold, I am alive for evermore, Amen; and have the keys of hell and of death.
Rev 1:8.

April 22

****
Blessed are ye, when men shall revile you, and persecute you, and shall say all manner of evil against you falsely, for my sake.

– Matthew 5:11
****

In 2009 a Christian nurse was suspended in the United Kingdom, just for politely asking to pray for one of her patients. Her request caused the displeasure, not of the patient involved, but instead her roommate, who lodged a complaint with the authorities, who in turn decided to suspend her, pending an investigation into her conduct. Though she was eventually reinstated, no matter how strong her faith was, in the initial stages of the matter her reaction would likely be that of shock and disappointment. Her suspension might initially have caused her some headaches – yes, even sleepless nights.

Indeed, the fact that we have decided to follow Christ does not mean we will necessarily be spared trouble – that we shall not be subject to the troubles and headaches that are characteristic of life on a fallen planet. I dare say, in fact, that we are even more prone to challenges compared to our peers in the world. Indeed, our calling may often place us at odds with the norms of society. We may involuntarily have to swim against the tide of society – and for the very reason that we want to uphold the tenets of our faith.

As we go about our daily chores today, I pray the Lord will give us the strength to withstand persecutions meted against us by virtue of our faith, however intense.

Stay blessed, fellow soldier of the Cross of Calvary.

APRIL 23

****
For the Lord God is a sun and shield.

– Psalm 84:11

****

David declares in this Psalm that the Lord God is his shield. In other words, he is proclaiming that Almighty God has built a metal device around him to protect him from blows, missiles or any dangerous objects directed against him!

With Almighty God, the Creator of heaven and earth shielding him from danger, David is able to go about his daily activities calm and collected. He is not going to invite trouble; but if despite his peaceful approach to life, the Enemy, out of sheer envy, malice, hatred, bitterness, venom, jealousy, etc., etc., decides to launch an unprovoked assault on him, he is not perturbed. Yes indeed, with the Ancient of Days as his protecting shield, David is assured that should the destroyer even decide to borrow from both the American and the Russian armies the most destructive weapons in their arsenal – laser-guided precision bombs, inter-continental ballistic missiles, bunker-penetration assault bombs – you can go on naming them – and aim them at him, he will not come to harm.

So fellow Christian soldier, let us, like the psalmist, face this day assured that no matter the destructive power the weapons the Enemy aiming at us carries, they cannot harm us, for indeed we have the Most High God as our shield!!

So "be strong and of a good courage, fear not, nor be afraid of them: for the LORD thy God, he it is that doth go with thee; he will not fail thee, nor forsake thee." Deuteronomy 31:6 (KJV)

APRIL 24

****

The LORD is my light and my salvation; whom shall I fear? the LORD is the strength of my life; of whom shall I be afraid? When the wicked, even mine enemies and my foes, came upon me to eat up my flesh, they stumbled and fell. Though an host should encamp against me, my heart shall not fear: though war should rise against me, in this will I be confident.

— **Psalm 27:1-3**

****

    Soldier of Christ, is the battle going against you?
    Is the enemy closing in on you?
    Are his fiery darts threatening you from all angles?
    Are his bullets whistling past you from all directions?
    Does it appear as if you'll soon be vanquished?
    You look all around you – there seems no hope of escape;
    You are caught up in enemy territory.
    You look left and right; backward and forward –
    All seem to have deserted you!
    You are despairing, despairing, despairing!
    You begin to wonder where the Commander-in-Chief the Lord of Lords
    He in whom you have placed all your hope is to be found.
    Stand firm, stand firm!
    Resign not, resign not!
    Soon, very soon, the rescuing hands
    Of the Invincible Lord
    Will appear from nowhere, to evacuate you from enemy territory.
    So do not lose heart embattled soldier of the Cross of Calvary.

April 25

****

Fear thou not; for I am with thee: be not dismayed; for I am thy God: I will strengthen thee; yea, I will help thee; yea, I will uphold thee with the right hand of my righteousness.

– Isaiah 41:10

****

I read the other day the story of a young girl who was travelling in a ship that was captained by her father. In the course of the journey, they encountered a terrible storm which threatened to capsize the ship. Whereas all around her became panicky the little girl maintained her calm. Asked by the others why she was not scared, her reply was: "Papa is at the helm; all will be well!"

My dear Christian friend, are your circumstances overwhelming you? You seem to be stranded in the midst of the huge Antarctic Ocean. In the midst of the biting cold, with temperatures several degrees below zero, you are freezing! You are lost, lost, lost. You cast your glance to the north and to the south, to the east and the west. Humanity is nowhere to be seen. When you need help most, mankind has deserted you.

I have a message for you, despairing Christian soldier: take courage and wait, for as sure as the African sun will appear in the skies at the dawn of a new day, so also will Heaven come your way.

Yes indeed, I want you to adopt the same attitude of the little girl, for indeed Papa Almighty God is in charge so the storm will never capsize your boat – no, it never will!

April 26

****

Yea, though I walk through the valley of the shadow of death, I will fear no evil: for thou art with me; thy rod and thy staff they comfort me

– Psalm 23:4

****

Cast your fears to the winds, dear fellow soldier of the cross of Calvary; no need to fear, dear sister, no need to fear, dear brother. Do not fear a possible credit crunch that may set in to wipe out all your savings; do not fear the cancer that threatens to attack you and cut short your life on earth; do not fear poverty; do not fear unemployment; do not fear anything – come what may! You might as well apply to the registry responsible for your area of residence to change your name to Miss/Mrs/Mr No Fears. Indeed, since you are journeying through life with the Lord who even the storms and the seas obey at your side, you may well travel bare-chested with the words 'no fears' boldly emblazoned on your chest for all to read!

Even should the most aggressive bear be staring you in the face, threatening to pounce on you at any moment, you could still wave the 'no fears' banner.

And surely, should you even be in the process of being swallowed by a giant whale – just as in the case of Jonah, yes, I can visualize your body being pulled gradually into its belly: your two legs are gone, your main body gradually vanishing, disappearing, and only your head is raging out of the belly of the destroyer! – even then I urge you to mobilize all the energy left in you and shout at the top of your voice for all the world to hear: no fears yesterday, no fears today, and no fears for evermore!

APRIL 27

****

Call upon me in the day of trouble: I will deliver thee, and thou shalt glorify me.

Psalm 50:15

****

Dear child of God, I can assure you that in response to your persistent calls on Heaven for help, the Lord of Heaven and earth indeed will arise and rebuke the problems, the challenges, the afflictions, etc., at war with you.

Get up, pick up a megaphone if you can lay hold of one, and declare at the top of your voice: "The Lord will arise on my behalf!" Yes indeed, He will!

Child of God, even if you have left all to serve the Lord; indeed, if you serve Him with all your heart, then rest assured that the Lord of Creation will arise on your behalf and rebuke the troubles confronting you, the problems threatening to choke you.

The world may count you the least amongst your fellow human beings – not counted among the wealthy, the influential, the prominent; neither among the educated nor the political elite.

You may, like myself, have been born into abject poverty; indeed, as in my case, a makeshift bathroom in one of the most impoverished areas on the globe might have served as the delivery suite where your eyes first saw the light of day! And indeed, you may find yourself on the lowest rung on the social ladder; yet the Lord of the whole universe, the King of Kings and Lord of Lords, He who is not impressed by the outside, He who looks on the inside and not the outside, will rise up to your calls for help!

So pick up courage, child of God, and wait on the rescuing Hands of our Loving Lord.

April 28

****

For we wrestle not against flesh and blood, but against principalities, against powers, against the rulers of the darkness of this world, against spiritual wickedness in high places.

– Ephesians 6:12-13

****

One day, as I sat down contemplating the ongoing battle raging between the Christian soldier and the Enemy, a scene, just as in a movie, flashed before my eyes. In the scene I saw the child of God in the form of a jetliner taxiing on the runway of an airport, preparing to take off. Pursuing the jetliner was a sports car boasting the most powerful engine the engineers at Ferrari, Mercedes, or BMW could ever come up with. At the wheel of the sports car was Satan! Jeered on by the spectators, Satan is giving the child of God a fierce chase. Indeed, the Evil One is pressing hard on the accelerator; the accelerator pedal is fully depressed. The monstrous engine of the sports car is racing at full throttle. Indeed, it looks as if it will soon overtake the jetliner.

Child of God, you are being pursued, pursued, pursued! I have a word for you, distressed soldier of the cross of Calvary! Rest assured, rest assured, friend, says the Lord your maker. Indeed, you might as well begin to give mocking gestures towards your enemy! Feel free to ridicule the driver of the sports car – for when push comes to shove, you can take to your wings and fly to escape the evil machinations of the Great Deceiver!

So, rest assured and enjoy this wonderful day ahead of you, my good Christian friend!

April 29

****

What? Know ye not that your body is the temple of the Holy Ghost which is in you, which ye have of God, and ye are not your own?

– 1 Corinthians 6:19

****

Now the Holy Spirit through the Apostle Paul is telling us that our respective bodies represent the *temple* of the Holy Spirit! My body is a *temple* of the Holy Spirit – that is an awesome, yes an amazing, indeed a mind-boggling assertion!

I am not trying to frighten anyone; neither do I want to exaggerate matters. The fact still remains that, sometimes, I am even afraid to assign the title "Christian" to myself. Why? You may ask. My answer is simple – Christianity is a high calling, yes a very high calling indeed. Now the Holy Father has sent His Holy spirit to dwell in us. As real soldiers of the Cross, our bodies are no longer ours, but the Lord's. This is an amazing fact. Now we know that the Lord is Holy and nothing impure can come near Him. So if the Holy Spirit is dwelling in us, then nothing impure should come near our respective bodies to render them impure. It's as if we were wearing a snow-white wedding gown – so dirt, filth, impurity, away, away with you! Go away, all impurity – never come near us!

May Almighty Father grant us the grace needed to uphold the good name of our calling as we go about our daily chores today – to the glory of His Mighty Name.

April 30

Thou therefore endure hardness, as a good soldier of Jesus Christ.

– 2 Timothy 2:3

There is a saying that "Life is War. Indeed, life on our fallen planet can pose challenges to its residents, believers and unbelievers alike."

There is a difference between the believer in Christ and the nonbeliever engaged in the "war of life" though. The believer in Christ is fighting on the side of a winning army. Indeed, the Lord we serve won the victory for us on the cross 2000 years ago. So even before the whistle is blown to signify the beginning of the conflict with the principalities seeking to devour us, victory is already assured.

That does not mean, however, that we may not, in the course of the battle with those bent on destroying us, receive some blows to our body. Don't underestimate the enemy, who has engaged us with determination in a fight in the boxing ring. Though assured of victory in the bout, we could, at every stage in the 12-round combat, suffer some considerable whipping from the opponent. It is even possible we could lose some of the rounds. At the end of the day, however, victory will be ours, friends. Victory will be ours, for indeed the moment our Lord cried "It is finished!" on Golgotha's mount 2000 years ago, His victory and our victory were forever established.

So, let us go out with all boldness to face the challenges of this glorious new day!

May 1

****

I will praise thee; for I am fearfully and wonderfully made: marvellous are thy works; and that my soul knoweth right well.

– Psalm 139:14

****

Sometimes when I am alone I reflect on the anatomy of my body. In such moments I begin to wonder, how come others have the nerve to question the existence of a Creator, even to hold the view that we came about as a result of mere chance?!

Consider the brain that gives us thought; the ears that help us hear the news of the day, good and bad; the eyes that help us see our environment – the beautiful roses, the boundless oceans, the mighty elephants; the heart that dutifully pumps blood to nourish our body systems and in so doing keeps us alive, etc., etc. – can all this intricate, all this elaborate, indeed all this complex intelligent design be the result of sheer coincidence?

Indeed, despite the changes in my personal and family fortunes, pleasant and unpleasant; despite the stormy and turbulent times of the present world; despite the disasters and catastrophes of the world – natural and man-made – indeed, in spite of the economic, political, social and all other upheavals we hear, see and read about in our day, I will , like the psalmist, continue to declare at the top of my voice: *I will praise thee; for I am fearfully and wonderfully made: marvellous are thy works; and that my soul knoweth right well.* —Psalm 139:14

May 2

****

I will say of the Lord, He is my refuge and my fortress.

– Psalm 91:2

****

Every creature seeks refuge in the hour of danger – the bird flies away to the thicket, the fox hastens to its hole, the squirrel seeks refuge on tree tops.

As far as humanity is concerned our only sure refuge is God Almighty. The reality though is that not everyone has come to this realisation.

Indeed, some individuals seek refuge in their wealth – money, property, material possessions. Putting trust in wealth, material possessions, is indeed like building on sand!!

Some have made their fiancées and partners their refuge. Please do not get me wrong. We need to be committed to our partners and also be able to share our anxieties and concerns with them. We must learn to put matters in perspective though. No matter how dedicated our spouses are to us, we must realize that they are also human beings. There have been instances when some have threatened to commit suicide – unfortunately have even committed suicide – at the thought of losing their partners.

Sadly, the tendency to look elsewhere for refuge instead of to Almighty God is not restricted to those who do not call on the name of the Lord our Righteousness. Indeed, some Christians, by their attitude, seem to create the impression that their pastors are equal if not even more powerful than the Master Himself! The servant claiming equality with or even superiority to the Master Himself! Yes indeed, some of us seem to create the impression that healing powers reside in our pastors instead of the Divine Himself

Dear Christian friend, instead of seeking worldly sanctuary in time of danger, let us rather flee to the safety of Jehovah, the Eternal Protector of His own. For surely He is the only sure refuge available on our fallen planet.

May 3

****

For you created my inmost being: you knit me together in my mother's womb.

– Psalm 139:13 (NIV)

****

If only those claiming there is no God would sit down to reflect. Yes indeed, if only they would pause for a moment to consider how God preserved them in their mother's womb as they lay there, helpless. If indeed the atheists, yes those who keep on publishing their ideas denying the existence of God, would give thought to the time when they lay helpless in their mother's womb!

Is it not indeed amazing what the womb, created by our Supreme Father, is capable of achieving? The womb of a woman, known as the uterus, when not pregnant measures about 8 cm in length, 5 cm in width and about 2.5 cm in thickness. The extent of expansion that this small mass of muscle undergoes in order to harbour the unborn child is simply incredible!

Several years ago, when I was residing in Hanover, Germany, a little German child took the nickname of the One-Million-Dollar Baby. This is how that child came to acquire that title:

The parents were holidaying in the U.S. when the highly pregnant visitor from Germany went into labour several weeks ahead of term. Eventually she delivered her baby in a hospital there. As might be expected, she was grateful to the hospital for the around-the-clock care accorded to her premature child. The shock soon came home to her, however. After her premature baby had spent a few weeks in the neo-natal unit, the hospital presented her with a bill near one million dollars! Imagine the consternation of parents if our Almighty Father demanded from them one million dollars for having utilised the womb He created to enable their offspring to develop.

My dear Christian friend, let us boldly proclaim our faith at every opportunity for we serve indeed an awesome God!

May 4

****

God is our refuge and strength, a very present help in trouble.

– Psalm 46:1

****

The Psalmist proclaims at the top of his voice that "God is an ever-present help in time of trouble" so His children need not worry.

While a student in Germany, one of my German mates invited me to his wedding in his hometown, about one hundred kilometres from Hanover where I was resident. I planned my journey in such a manner as to arrive at my destination about an hour prior to the church service. I travelled in a rented car. The vehicle was barely six months old, so I was confident it would take me to my destination without any mechanical problems developing. Nevertheless, I was about twenty minutes' drive from my destination when I heard a strange noise emanating from the back of the vehicle! I pulled to a stop on the relatively quiet road. I realised then to my dismay that one of the back tyres was punctured – by a sharp object on the road, perhaps.

As might be expected the almost new vehicle had on board a spare tyre as well as the tools needed to change the damaged tyre. At that moment in my life, however, I had no idea how to do that! Yet another problem I soon became aware of – there was no emergency station in sight from where I could call for help (the incident dates back to the mid-1980s – I personally had not heard of mobile phones at that time!).

Thankfully Almighty God, who provides ever-present help in times of trouble, was aware of my predicament, even before it happened and had dispatched help to my rescue.

Indeed, just as I got out of my vehicle, another vehicle coming from the direction I was heading towards arrived at the scene.

On seeing my problem, the driver pulled to a stop and offered his assistance. Within a matter of minutes he was able to change the damaged tyre. "Goodbye and safe journey!" He shook my hand and returned to his vehicle. Moments later he was out of sight.

Our Loving God is indeed an ever-present help in trouble! Should you, my dear Christian friend, experience a "breakdown" as you go about your activities today, I pray Him to quickly dispatch His angels your way to render much needed assistance.

Stay blessed, my fellow Christian warrior!

May 5

****

Be patient therefore, brethren, unto the coming of the Lord. Behold, the husbandman waiteth for the precious fruit of the earth, and hath long patience for it, until he receive the early and latter rain. Be ye also patient; stablish your hearts: for the coming of the Lord draweth nigh.

– James 5:7-8

****

Are you losing your patience, embattled Christian soldier?
Are you getting weary of waiting on the Lord?
Have you been wondering when the Lord shall come your way?
"I have waited and waited in vain!"
Thus I hear you say in a spirit of resignation!
I have come to tell you, child of God,
to hold on, hold on and don't lose heart,
for to Him in whom you have trusted,
a thousand years are like a day that passes away.
No, He has not forgotten you;
surely He will soon turn your night into day.

Patience, patience, child of God!
True, there seems no end to your woes,
no end to your calamities.
You have been calling on the Lord all this long for help but He seems not to hear.
The Son of God appears to be too far away to hear your silent prayer.
Yet I say, patience, child of God, patience!

Picture the Lord sitting in a boat with you –
in the midst of the storm He seems to be asleep!
No, He that was cleft for you never sleeps nor slumbers!
Lift your hands up!
Through persistent prayer draw His attention to your plight.
No, it is never too late, never too late to draw His attention.
Yes, He will surely come your way.
So rest assured, and face your troubles, challenges, problems and what-have-you with renewed confidence.

May 6

****

Let all bitterness, and wrath, and anger, and clamour, and evil speaking, be put away from you, with all malice: And be ye kind one to another, tender-hearted, forgiving one another, even as God for Christ's sake hath forgiven you.

– **Ephesians 4:31-32**

****

No matter how deeply others might offend us, we are called upon by the Lord of Heaven and Earth to forgive them. It is a fact of life that it is not always easy to forgive those who hurt us. I remember how a business associate, someone I trusted, abused my trust and defrauded me of a substantial sum of money.

Does the Lord really call on me to forgive such a fellow? Of course, He who created us knows what He is talking about when He implores us to do exactly that. He placed the immune system in our body to defend the body against the invasion of germs and other parasites. It has been established by medical science that bitterness, an unforgiving spirit, hatred, cares, worry, stress, etc., can weaken our immune system – yes, the body defences.

That must not come as a surprise. Do you remember the last time you felt aggrieved by someone – your partner, brother, sister, friend, colleague? You felt so angered by the person involved that you spent the whole night grumbling over the matter. Mind you, at the time you were struggling to sleep as a result of your grumblings, the individual concerned might have been fast, fast asleep. That individual might very likely wake up the next day, refreshed by the thorough sleep. You, on the other hand, may well have risen the next day with a dejected face, suffering from the effect of the poor sleep of the previous night. This state of mind, should it persist for long, could result in the weakening of our immune system. Thus, at the end of the day, it is in our interests to forgive those who hurt or causes us pain.

Let us, my dear Christian friend, pray for the grace to enable us to forgive our foes, however deeply we feel offended by them.

MAY 7

The thief cometh not, but for to steal, and to kill, and to destroy: I am come that they might have life, and that they might have it more abundantly.

– John 10:10

When I was growing up in my little village in Ghana, we raised poultry at home, not for commercial purposes, but for our own use. We did not confine our birds to their chicken coops or hen houses during the day; instead, we permitted them to roam about freely.

That practice exposed them to two main dangers.

Firstly, though the road that passed through the village was not particularly busy with traffic, vehicular movement was nevertheless sufficient to pose a danger to our birds. Not infrequently some of them were run over by passing vehicles and crushed into pieces.

Our birds faced danger that originated not only on land; they were also subjected to threats to their lives that came from the air. Our area abounded with hawks that hunted our birds from above. The hawks were indeed a menace to our poultry. They would, as if from nowhere, appear in the sky, make a forceful dive downwards towards their prey, grasp the poor bird in their claws and fly away, just as swiftly as they arrived. The hunting expedition of the 'thief' from the air was executed so briskly and with such precision, it left the human inhabitants hardly any time for counter attack.

Today's verse points to a thief who comes to steal, kill and destroy. Oh, how many millions have become victims of the great thief!

Lets us, fellow Soldiers of the Cross of Calvary, be thankful to our Commander-in-Chief for the protection He offers us from dangers innumerable that we are exposed to on the battlefield of life. Surely, so long as we stay close to Him, no weapon formed against us will proper.

May 8

****
Bear ye one another's burdens, and so fulfil the law of Christ.

– **Galatians 6:2**
****

My journey to the Hanover Medical School in Germany went through West Berlin. I lived there as an asylum seeker. My time as a refugee in the city was challenging. As an asylum seeker I was neither allowed to work nor study; the fact that I faced an uncertain future, with the prospect of being deported back to my native Ghana, added to my woes.

Our Loving Father did not leave me alone in my gloomy situation. Instead His mysterious Hands led me to some of His sons and daughter living in the city, to help make life there bearable.

One of them was Rhea. At the time of our meeting she was about 65 – she had retired from her work as a hospital doctor a few years before. At the time I got to know her, she occupied a large apartment which boasted of at least six large rooms, excluding the kitchen and the toilet. She lived alone. As I later learnt, she had no children of her own. This background information might lead one to ask why she chose to rent such a large apartment. The fact is, she saw it as part of her Christian calling to invite others, particularly Christians, who for whatever reason had nowhere to live or were experiencing personal challenges, to stay with her for a while for a change.

When she learnt of my plight she invited me from time to time to stay with her. She did not only open her home to me in my time of need, she also on occasions provided monetary and material assistance (in the form of new clothing).

Dear Christian friend, you may be reading theses lines at a time of dire financial need. You may indeed be left with virtually nothing to exist on. I pray the Lord to lead you to your "Rhea" to offer you the needed help. Until that happens, I urge you to hold on to the Good Shepherd and do not allow poverty to force you to give up your faith.

May 9

****

Then Peter said, Silver and gold have I none; but such as I have give I thee: In the name of Jesus Christ of Nazareth rise up and walk. And he took him by the right hand, and lifted him up: and immediately his feet and ankle bones received strength. And he leaping up stood, and walked, and entered with them into the temple, walking, and leaping, and praising God.

– Acts 3:6-8

****

What an amazing example of Divine Intervention! No need for the taking of clinical history on the part of Peter, no need for him to perform a clinical examination, no need for him to request a blood examination; no need for x-ray, ultrasound scan, CT scan; no need for MRI scan; no need for surgery! All that Peter needed to do was to invoke the Name above all Names and command the victim of disease to get up and walk.

Let us ponder the matter for a moment. At the name of Jesus, instant strength returned to the limbs of the afflicted man, an individual who had been paralysed since birth! I can imagine the muscles and bones of his lower limbs shrinking and weakening from years of disuse and inactivity. The shrinking of the muscles in turn would have led to the reduction in the sizes of the nerves and vessels supplying them.

Enter Peter upon the scene. He commands the victim of disease to get up and walk in Jesus' name, and instantly the bones and muscles are strengthened. The vessels and nerves on their part increase in size and length to cope with the new situation.

Fellow Christian soldier, let us be proud of our calling for we do indeed serve an awesome God.

May 10

> **So we fasted and besought our God for this: and he was intreated of us.**
>
> – Ezra 8:23

A period came in my life when I was very distressed about the prospect of being deported from Germany back to my native Ghana to face an uncertain future.

During that period my mind was so tensed that even comforting words from the Bible seemed to lack the power to penetrate the dark wall around me. Though I had been fasting occasionally, I decided to resort to regular fasting and prayer. Soon I realised how invaluable was the help that came from fasting in situations like that. I must stress the fact that I did not embark on my fast primarily to please God – how could I indeed expect to please the Almighty with my fast!

To put it bluntly, I did so not to go crazy! So intense was the sense of anguish on my mind.

Once I engaged in a fast I was able to reach a state of mental purity and peace. With the tension on my mind gone, I seemed to be over and above all the problems around me. It was such a wonderful state of mind that I often felt reluctant to break the fast at the end of the day.

Even now my personal belief is that God does not need the fast of His children. It is His children rather who need the fast to attain the state of mind that helps them draw close to Him in their prayers. Fasting, if you like, helps to dissipate the clouds of resistance that would otherwise hamper the transmission of our prayer waves to Heaven.

My Dear Christian soldier, I do not know your personal situation. You may have a medical condition that may not be conducive to fasting. I wouldn't recommend a fast in such a situation. Otherwise, you may consider combining your prayers with a fast. It has been helpful to me so I am humbly recommending the same to you.

May 11

> The name of the LORD is a strong tower: the righteous runneth into it, and is safe.
>
> – Proverbs 18:10

Imagine my dear Christian friend you are a fierce opponent of the government of a little country somewhere on the globe, indeed a weak and impoverished country. In the face of the wanton corruption going on in your country, you have been publishing article upon article criticizing the government. The president of that country, intent on showing you where power lies, dispatches some of his security forces to arrest you. Just as they are under way, someone calls you on your mobile phone to warn you about the impending arrest. Sensing danger, you make it through the back door of your home and begin running as fast as you can towards to the US consulate in the capital.

Somehow the agents of the president get the news of your flight and give you chase. Just as they are about to grasp you, you manage at the very last minute to enter the premises of the US Embassy. On producing your ID card and telling your story, you are offered sanctuary. Safe within the walls of the compound of the embassy of the most powerful country on earth, you look through the glass window of the consulate building and spot your enemies on the street, retreating, anger visibly written all over their faces. In the safety of your refuge, you, who minutes earlier feared for your life, have the audacity to make mocking gestures towards them!

If we can trust in earthly refuge, let us not fear the principalities and powers of darkness up against us my dear Christian friend, for we have a surer refuge under the wings of the Most High God.

MAY 12

But the God of all grace, who hath called us unto his eternal glory by Christ Jesus, after that ye have suffered a while, make you perfect, stablish, strengthen, settle you.
– 1 Peter 5:10

May the light of the Everlasting Father,
the beams originating from the Source of all light,
brighten our horizon and illuminate our path this day.
May the Eternal light overcome
the darkness surrounding us
and give us hope for today and the days ahead.

May the light of the Everlasting Father
shine on our homes this day
to guide the paths of all the inhabitants
and protect them from evil.
May the Light of the Everlasting Father
be a torch to lead us and our whole household
this day on the path of righteousness.

May the light of the Everlasting Father shine on us
and dissipate the clouds looming on our horizon;
may the Everlasting light shine on us abundantly
and make us a source reflecting
His rays to illuminate the paths of all
who come in contact with us.
So let our light shine amongst men
that they may give glory to the Heavenly Father.

May 13

****

God is our refuge and strength, a very present help in trouble. Therefore will not we fear, though the earth be removed, and though the mountains be carried into the midst of the sea; though the waters thereof roar and be troubled, though the mountains shake with the swelling thereof.

– Psalm 46:1-3

****

The Psalmist is declaring that even though the earth be removed, and though the mountains be carried into the midst of the sea, we need not fear. He goes on to state that "though the waters thereof roar and be troubled, though the mountains shake with the swelling thereof" he will still not be scared.

To appreciate to the very full the message the psalmist is seeking to convey, let us imagine the force that a large haulage lorry loaded to the full with, say, bags of cement, is capable of generating should it be let loose at the peak of a high mountain and be allowed to crash into an ocean beneath it.

You and I, let us go a step further to picture in our minds the situation whereby Mount Everest, all of a sudden, is uprooted from its very foundations and tossed into the sea. What a scene that would be – awesome, simply terrific!

I got a taste of what the situation I have just referred to might be like when an earthquake of the magnitude 5.2 hit England in the early hours of 27th February 2008. My goodness, it was terrible! The earth that provides the support for our movements, the very foundation of our dwelling, our bastion, began to shake and rumble – like the rumbling made when a jumbo jet touches down and begins to decelerate on the runway.

The psalmist is proclaiming at the top of his voice to the whole world that should the earth shake and rumble as a result of an earthquake of magnitude 10 plus on the Richter Scale, causing Mount Kilimanjaro to be uprooted and carried into the sea, he will not fear.

Whatever the problems and burden confronting us today, we should not let them weigh us down. Instead let us bring them before the Great High God, yes before He who has the power and authority to move mountains, however huge!

May 14

****

And it came to pass after these things, that his master's wife cast her eyes upon Joseph; and she said, Lie with me. But he refused, and said unto his master's wife, Behold, my master wotteth not what is with me in the house, and he hath committed all that he hath to my hand; There is none greater in this house than I; neither hath he kept back anything from me but thee, because thou art his wife.

– Genesis 39:7-9

****

As we wait on the Lord to fulfil His promise in our life, I pray that we learn from Joseph's experience and not take short cuts to success. Indeed, Joseph could have yielded to temptation and taken short cuts with the aim of achieving his goal – but no, he would not depart from principle, come what may!

It is said that human nature has the tendency to follow the path of least resistance. We are tempted to say things like "everyone is doing it so I will also follow suit!"

When tempted by Potiphar's wife, Joseph could also have come up with an argument like: "Well, if she won't leave me alone, then I might as well cave in. After all, it's not my fault that things have come to this point. If Almighty God did not prevent my brothers from selling me into slavery, and if on top of all that He has not prevented the tempting approaches of such an attractive lady, then that's it! I have no choice but to cave in to the unbearable emotional and psychological pressure being exerted on me."

He might even have looked beyond the short-term sensual pleasure he would obtain from his deed to the long-term advantages his affair with the mistress of his master might have brought him. But no, Joseph would not give in to enchantment. No, he would not compromise. His motto was, "No compromise in good times, no compromise in difficult times – no compromise on waking up, no compromise when going about his daily tedious chores, and no compromise when retiring to bed."

Dear Christian friend, let's pray the Lord to help us stand by His principles when faced with tough and difficult choices!

May 15

****

Goliath walked out toward David with his shield bearer ahead of him, sneering in contempt at this ruddy-faced boy. "Am I a dog," he roared at David, "that you come at me with a stick?" And he cursed David by the names of his gods. "Come over here," Goliath yelled, "and I'll give your flesh to the birds and wild animals!"

– 1 Samuel 17:41-44

****

Child of God, I can see in my mind's eye Goliath charging on you. For what reason, you may wonder? It's true, you have done him no wrong—indeed, nothing to warrant the assault. His attack is unprovoked, I agree, totally baseless!

You are living your life in peace. You are working hard to cater for yourself and your family, standing up at cockcrow and working all day, indeed shedding sweat to earn an honest wage. You have no ill will towards anyone. Certainly, you are not thinking evil towards anyone. You thought others would reciprocate your goodwill towards them and leave you in peace, but no! Well, unfortunately, the spirit of envy, jealousy, backbiting, does not understand diplomatic language. So even though you have nothing against them, they have declared war against you!

So, Goliath the enemy is launching an assault not against you only, but also your family, your business, yes everything dear to you. Stay calm and collected my dear Christ friend. No panic; no fears. Hear the Lord in whom you have placed your trust declare assuredly: "Do not be afraid of their faces, for I am with you to deliver you," (Jeremiah 1:8)

For sure, the Lord will fight your fight for you, Just as He did in the case of David—so rest assured and maintain your calm, precious child of God!

May 16

****

He will not suffer thy foot to be moved: he that keepeth thee will not slumber. Behold, he that keepeth Israel shall neither slumber nor sleep

– Psalm 121:3-4

****

Dear Christian friends, we serve a God who never slumbers! Yet lo and behold, the moment trouble begins to brew around us, the moment danger begins to knock on our doors, and yes, for sure, when we are in the midst of the ferocious sandstorms of life and our view is not only blocked but our eyes begin to burn and hurt, we tend to create the impression we serve a God who slumbers and sleeps from time to time!

By our behaviour and attitude, we seem to be under the impression that our God is like the watchman who, having vowed in the presence of his employer to keep awake around the clock, begins to doze off minutes after his master has left the scene!

Does the problem stem from the fact that our human mind cannot comprehend how it can be possible for someone to keep awake all the time, second after second, minute after minute, hour after hour, day after day, year a after year, through all eternity?

Indeed, how tired and weary do I feel the day after I have done an overnight duty! Throughout the course of the day, I not only feel exhausted, I also lose my concentration. In the same way we seem to imagine that Almighty God is just as frail as common humanity.

Dear Christian friends, let us not grow weary of waiting on the Lord. The delay may be long and distressing; still, we should not grow weary for we are waiting on no other than the Lord Jesus! Yes indeed, let us gather strength, embattled soldiers of the Cross, and keep the vigilant watch! Our Commander-in-Chief has indeed been tried and proven faithful under all circumstances! Come what may, He surely will visit his own to turn our situation around.

So, let us encourage one another and hold on to the very end!

May 17

****

He answered and said, Whether he be a sinner or no, I know not: one thing I know, that, whereas I was blind, now I see.

– John 9:25

****

In our day, great effort is undertaken by those who live in spiritual darkness to discredit the faith. Among other things they dispute the fact of creation, the virgin birth; the resurrection – the list goes on.

Satan the archenemy never rests. Oh, indeed, he is busy at work today, even right now. His main aim? To discredit JESUS OUR LORD. He is ready to use whoever is ready to serve as an agent in his diabolic scheme to slander the Holy Name of the Sinless One. Sadly, multitudes have fallen prey and continue to fall prey to his insinuations.

We find them everywhere: in the media; in politics; in the academic world –academicians and experts they may be called, yet they go about with open chests, from conference to conference, from continent to continent, spreading their theses and theories to discredit the Lord, my Strength, in order to cast doubt on the divinity of Jesus the Lord.

My Dear Christian soldier, I urge you to join me in prayer for these wretched and miserable souls, whose minds have been taken over by the enemy, that they will gain their freedom and come to know that truth, the truth that will set them free.

May 18

****
For ye shall go out with joy, and be led forth with peace: the mountains and the hills shall break forth before you into singing, and all the trees of the field shall clap their hands.

– Isaiah 55:12
****

I hear you child of God battling with all sorts of life challenges, after reading through those words of comfort and cheer state bluntly:

"Well, what I am going through is just the opposite of what is expressed here. No signs of the mountains and hills singing and no signs of trees clapping with joy! I have no job, I am unable to pay my bills; my health is not good – my back aches terribly; I am plagued with menstrual pain; as if that is not enough I am also afflicted with kidney stones causing me excruciating pain!

"Yes indeed, I feel like I am stuck in the middle of a long tunnel; I am surrounded by darkness, yes, darkness so deep it seems palpable! Ahead of me and behind me; to the left and to the right – zero visibility! No mountains, no hills in sight to break forth into singing; no trees in view to clap their hands to cheer me on!"

My heart goes out to you, suffering child of God. One thing I can assure you though – the words of cheer of today's verse is not meant for a selected few; no, the words of cheer spoken under inspiration by Prophet Isaiah are meant for every child of God.

It may indeed be a while before you reach the end of your tunnel, before you emerge out of the deep abyss to behold the singing mountains and clapping trees. Until that happens, I pray for Divine Grace and favour to help you endure until the dawn of the new and bright day.

So muster courage, despairing child of God and don't throw in the towel in the face of the seemingly insurmountable odds.

MAY 19

God is our refuge and strength, a very present help in trouble.

– Psalm 46:1

I do not want to speak for the composer of the Psalm, but I guess he deliberately chose the pronoun, *our*, instead of, *my*, because he thought he could gain universal approval for his stance. To him God's presence is so obvious, he could not imagine anyone disputing the fact of His existence, just as no one will dispute the essential role of oxygen for life on earth. Indeed, as far as he is concerned, the fact he is expressing is unequivocal, unquestionable, straightforward, explicit!

Of course, we know in our day that multitudes reject the existence of God. I can imagine some among such a group of people wishing that they could bring the composer of the psalm back to life and, with eyes boiling with rage, challenge him to his face: "Why dare you proclaim God is Our Refuge and Strength! That amounts to false generalization, that is going against the rules of political correctness, against respect for the concept of religious tolerance. We reserve the right to summon you before a court of law to request the Law Lords to force you to retract your words. You may indeed have your God as your refuge; but how dare you speak for us!"

To that the psalmist would likely respond as follows: "Sorry about that, ladies and gentlemen. I really thought commonsense was all that is needed for one to grasp what I am driving at. It looks as if for reasons best known to yourselves, you have decided to throw commonsense to the dogs! Well, you may deny the fact that God is *your* refuge – as far as I am concerned, however, God Zebaoth is my refuge and strength. Nothing, not even the threat of persecution, can alter my stance."

Dear Christian Soldiers, let us pray to the Lord to open the eyes of those who, despite the obvious evidence pointing to His existence, still reject Him, that they may see and behold his awesome presence in their lives.

MAY 20

****
Seek ye first the Kingdom of God, and his righteousness; and all these things shall be added unto you.

– Matthew 6:33

****

If at last we have found the Kingdom of God;
if after years of wandering in the wilderness,
we have at last arrived at the oases of life,
Let us hold on to Him, my friend,
Let us hold on to Him, my sister,
Let us hold on to Him, my brother.

If at last we have found the Kingdom of God;
if after spending all our years looking for the truth,
we have at last arrived at the Cross of Golgatha,
Let us not allow anything – poverty, disease, personal misfortune or
any kind of calamity to draw us away from the only Source of Life.

If by the grace of God we have been privileged to experience
the Light that shines in the darkness of this world,
let us hold on firmly to Him, no matter what the present or future may bring,
for we have found a precious Kingdom,
the Kingdom that will last for ever.

Some are holding on to the kingdom of riches,
others to the kingdom of fame;

others are clinging to the kingdom of glamour,
but the kingdoms of this world shall pass away.
Only that One Kingdom,
the Kingdom built on the Rock of Ages shall evermore abide.
So dear child of God, let us cast away all that will hamper us
and hold on to the Saviour Jesus Christ.

Yes indeed, if by God's grace we have at last found
the Kingdom of God, let us, fellow Christian soldier,
not allow anything of this world to tempt us off course;
Instead let us hold on to the end,
so together with the Apostle Paul, we may declare–
we have fought the good fight, we have finished the race,
we have kept the faith.

MAY 21

****

For I reckon that the sufferings of this present time are not worthy to be compared with the glory which shall be revealed in us

– Romans 8:18

****

Today's meditation is devoted in particular to Christian soldiers battling with diseases – minor as well as life-threatening.

As you lie in your hospital bed contemplating your situation, the ailment afflicting you, the terrible diagnosis proclaimed by the doctors, the thought going through your mind is – Why me, why me, Lord? Why not allow the cup of affliction to pass me?

Yes, as you lie in your hospital bed battling the serious disease that is threatening to cut your life short, serious doubts have arisen in your mind as to the kindness and goodness of the Lord in whom you have believed. Why has He allowed you to face the prospect of leaving this world at such a young age? Who will take care of your little children when you are gone?

Dear suffering child of God, I am deeply touched by your situation. Indeed, I wish I could provide suitable answers to the issues you have raised. But I am mortal just like you! How can we mortals who today are and tomorrow gone with the wind read the mind of the Almighty?

Still, I dare speak some words of comfort into your ears, you severely wounded warrior of Christ: In the face of the ferocious battle raging, yes, in the face of the boisterous winds fiercely whirling, threatening to capsize the boat you are sailing in, be assured that the Good and Faithful Friend in whom you have placed your trust will never desert you. In the past He has seen His faithful ones through storms too numerous to number. Today He accompanies His loving ones as they tread the valley of the shadow of death.

Forever He will be the refuge and strength of all who run to Him for cover – so cheer up and face your tomorrow with joyful expectation, knowing that He holds your hand through the valley of shadows and that it is He who pilots your boat through the storms of life. So be of good cheer, embattled Christian warrior.

MAY 22

****

For I am the LORD**, I change not; therefore ye sons of Jacob are not consumed.**

– **Malachi 3:6**

****

Empires have come and gone, but only the empire of God Zebaoth, the God who never changes, shall exist for ever. Did those who lived at the peak of the Roman empire ever imagine it could collapse?

Should those who lived at the zenith of the British Empire come back to life today, how amazed will they be to find the role, now merely ceremonial, that the head of that empire plays in today's world!

Let us even consider the recent past. When I arrived in West Berlin in 1982 and saw with my own eyes the Berlin Wall and the East German soldiers guarding it at several positions from the eastern territory, when the Soviet Union was mightily controlling the territories on the eastern side of the iron curtain dividing Europe, who could envisage that one day the Berlin Wall would crumble and with it the whole of the Soviet Union?

In the same way, which one of us can imagine what will become of the so-called superpowers of our day? Anything man-made is temporal; only the Power that created everything seen and unseen remains everlasting.

So my dear Christian friend, let us put our trust in nothing but the Unchangeable Great High God.

MAY 23

****
Wherefore God also hath highly exalted him, and given him a name which is above every name: That at the name of Jesus every knee should bow, of things in heaven, and things in earth, and things under the earth; And that every tongue should confess that Jesus Christ is Lord, to the glory of God the Father.

– Philippians 2:9-11
****

The other day, I heard about the case of a soldier from my native Ghana who served with the United Nations Interim Force in Lebanon (UNIFIL). Prior to his departure for Lebanon, he sought protection from a Juju priest. The witch doctor gave him a necklace that he was to wear throughout his tour of duty.

One day, during his stay, he accompanied other members of the UN contingent on a sightseeing tour of the Holy Land. As the story goes, when they got to the site of the empty tomb of Christ, all of a sudden the necklace that was supposed to offer him protection was torn apart by an invisible hand – torn to pieces! Juju power confronted by Divine power had no choice but to take to its heels and flee in panic. For the visiting soldier from Ghana, the day of salvation had come, for at that very moment he made the decision of his life – to follow the King of Kings and Lord of Lords!

I want to stress the fact that I am unable to verify whether the story is true or not. Nevertheless, should it come as a surprise if indeed Juju power was subjected to such humiliation at a Christian holy site? Not at all, for indeed at the Name of Mighty Jesus, every knee should bow, of things in heaven, and things on earth, and things under the earth!

My dear Christian friends, let us be proud of our calling and not be ashamed to confess the hope of our salvation at every opportunity, for indeed we serve an awesome God.

Have a blessed and fruitful day, my fellow Christian warrior.

May 24

****

Likewise, I say unto you, there is joy in the presence of the angels of God over one sinner that repenteth.

– Luke 15:10

****

Today's meditation is dedicated to the New Convert:

You have just made a decision to follow Christ the Lord. As the angels of Heaven are rejoicing at your decision, may I also welcome you home, my dear Christian friend.

I want to thank the Lord of heaven and earth for calling you home. I also want to congratulate you for your decision, indeed your bold decision to leave the world behind and embark on the exciting journey towards the New Jerusalem.

Perhaps you were called home after you had come to the end of your road. Perhaps you were called under less dramatic circumstances. Whatever the circumstances that led to your decision, one thing you can be certain of – you have made the right choice. Your Christian walk can be compared with the journey of the Israelites from Egypt to Canaan. You have indeed left the world behind and heading for the New Jerusalem.

I do not know what characterized your previous life – maybe you were addicted to alcoholic, to drugs, to sex, to pornography? Whatever the state from which you were called, I pray the Lord to send His Holy Spirit into your heart to help you in your war against the flesh.

Keep close to the Lord and victory shall be yours, for He tells us in John 6:37-40 that "All that the Father giveth me shall come to me; and him that cometh to me I will in no wise cast out."

May 25

****

When Jesus had lifted up himself, and saw none but the woman, he said unto her, Woman, where are those thine accusers? hath no man condemned thee? She said, No man, Lord. And Jesus said unto her, Neither do I condemn thee: go, and sin no more.

– John 8:10-11

****

The message of salvation is not only a feel-good message; we must also realise that it can be a radical one, one that requires us to examine our lives, one that calls for spiritual discipline, one that calls for a radical break with the past. That in my opinion is one of the reasons the Christian has been referred to as a soldier.

We are not politicians – yes, politicians seeking political office, who in the bid to gain as many votes as possible engage in political manoeuvring, saying this at one rally, promising that at the other rally, editing, polishing, reviewing our statements constantly. to appeal to voters, yes to gain more votes.

Neither are we diplomats – official representatives of our countries, envoys who have to choose our words carefully wherever we speak on behalf of our respective countries to avoid conflict, yes to display our countries in a proper light to the rest of the world.

We are rather soldiers, soldiers on the battlefield of life. As soldiers engaged in active warfare, we need to be vigilant at all times. In the midst of the fierce battle raging, yes with the bullets whistling past in all directions, we have no choice but to be eagle-eyed and on red alert – allowing for no complacency, no compromises, no parleying with the things of the flesh!

We are, by His Grace, saved from our sin; we should however resist the urge to return to them.

May the Blessing of the Holy One accompany us in all that we set out to do today.

May 26

****

Then said Jesus unto them again, Verily, verily, I say unto you, I am the door of the sheep. All that ever came before me are thieves and robbers: but the sheep did not hear them. I am the door: by me if any man enter in, he shall be saved, and shall go in and out, and find pasture.

– John 10:7-9

****

Some try various means, philosophies, lifestyles, teachings, etc., to find peace. They may succeed for a while, but such lifestyles, ideals, teachings, insights, etc., are food for the brain, the mind—unable to penetrate the heart to cause any changes, to remould the individual, yes to free the individual, for anything man-made is grounded on sand.

As the Lord declared to Nicodemus, such individuals need to be born again; indeed, they need a remoulding of their hearts; if they have not been born again, they have not experienced the new moulding of the heart—the change that will enable them to love rather than to hate, to forgive rather than to seek revenge.

Let us pray the Lord for the strength, yes the energy to bring the lost to the Door of Doors, the Door that alone can set them free, free from malice, anger, bitterness, back-biting; yes indeed, the door that opens the way to hope and everlasting Life.

May 27

****
What doth it profit, my brethren, though a man say he hath faith, and have not works? can faith save him? If a brother or sister be naked, and destitute of daily food, and one of you say unto them, Depart in peace, be ye warmed and filled; notwithstanding ye give them not those things which are needful to the body; what doth it profit? Even so faith, if it hath not works, is dead, being alone.

– James 2:14-17
****

In May 1982 I arrived in West Berlin. Later I applied to various Universities for the chance to study medicine. As part of the application process I was asked to provide proof of financial assistance. Although citizens as well as foreigners did not have to pay for tuition, everyone had to pay for their upkeep. How could I get someone to issue that vital letter?

The Lord led me to Kurt, a German pastor I had got to know during my stay in the city. Without hesitating, he agreed to issue such a letter. He did not only issue the requested letter—when my application was granted and I began my studies, he "put his money where his mouth was" by offering tangible financial assistance.

Dear Christian soldier battling with poverty and need, I pray Almighty God to send your "Kurt" to your home to provide needed assistance in your time of need. As you await the arrival of your angel, I pray Almighty Father to give you the strength to endure your present woes. So stay strong, poverty-stricken child of God.

MAY 28

****

Then Pharaoh said to Joseph, "I am Pharaoh, but without your word no one will lift hand or foot in all Egypt."

– Genesis 41:44

****

We are all familiar with the story of Joseph, how Almighty God turned him from Prisoner to Prime Minister in Egypt.

My friend, when God raises His hand to bless us, He can turn us for example from a poor student to a professor, from a street beggar to a millionaire, indeed from a commoner to a princess, the bride of His Royal, Royal Highness!

I do not have such an extraordinary turn-around event like Joseph's to report and talk about. Still, I would like to share one of my many turn-around experiences with you – not to blow my trumpet before the whole world, but rather to strengthen your faith, fellow soldier of the Cross.

In August, 1984, I was facing deportation as an Asylum seeker from West Berlin. My visa was due to expire in the third week of the month. In the end I escaped deportation at the very last moment through dramatic circumstance that space will not permit me to report here.

Shortly thereafter I matriculated at the Hannover Medical School and was issued a student's visa. Not long after obtaining the visa, the immigration authorities – the same authority that was seeking to deport me – in their desperate search for a translator for the Twi language (spoken in Ghana), contacted the Medical School authorities to find out if they had a student from Ghana who could serve that purpose. Eventually I became their part-time translator.

One moment a refugee threatened with deportation by the immigration authorities, the next moment a translator, helping the same authorities track a drug smuggling ring!

Dear Christian friend, we do indeed serve a turn-around God so we need not fear, come what may!

May 29

The Lord is on my side; I will not fear: what can man do unto me?

– Psalm 118:6

In the little village Mpintimpi, and also in several parts of the rural areas of my native Ghana, when the chief, the head of the community, wants to convey an important message to the rest of the community, he dispatches his "gong-gong beater" on an errand through the streets of the settlement to broadcast the news.

Kon-kon; kon-kon; kon-kon – he beats hard on his gong.

"M-p-i-n-t-i-m-p-i-f-o-e!!" ("Fellow residents of Mpintimpi"), he screams at the top of his voice. "I extend warm greetings from Nana [title of a chief]. He has asked me to pass such-and-such messages on to you!"

Kon-kon; kon-kon! – thus he beats his gong again to signify the end of the announcement.

He then moves on. After a distance of about 50 metres he stops, beats his gong once again and repeats the message. From there he walks another 50 or so metres and repeats the ritual. And so, on and on he goes, moving along the streets of the settlement beating his gong and broadcasting the message of the chief to the ears of everyone in every corner of the community.

In the same manner the composer of Psalm 118 is declaring on the top of his voice that "The LORD *is* on my side; I will not fear: what can man do unto me?"

The Lord is certainly on our side so let us pray to Him to help us overcome fear, depression, low self-esteem; yes, let us pray to our Loving Father to help us overcome all the negative thoughts that weigh us down, that sap our energy and make us tearful. Let us instead mobilize strength and energy and keep on waving the Christian flag.

May 30

****

Why art thou cast down, O my soul? and why art thou disquieted within me? hope in God: for I shall yet praise him, who is the health of my countenance, and my God.

– Psalm 43:5

****

Is the darkness engulfing you so thick as to be palpable, yes, so thick you cannot find your way out, leading you to stumble and fall several times?

Have you spent all your resources, child of God, and are left with nothing? Are you indeed virtually penniless with nothing to live on?

Are you stranded at a bus stop with no money left on you to enable you to continue your journey?

Does it feel like you are running out of time? Is the flight taking you to your destination about to take off without you? You hear the final call for passengers to proceed to board the plane. You are getting nervous, nervous, nervous! You have taken a look at you watch. You wonder why the Lord who is to accompany you on your journey is not turning up. Is He stuck in the busy rush hour traffic? Or has the vehicle conveying him to the airport perhaps suffered a breakdown?

Dear Christian friend whose soul is downcast as a result of the seemingly insurmountable problems confronting you, I urge you to get up and cast away your fears. No need for panic my friend, no need for alarm, no need for agitation.

Indeed, no matter the circumstances facing you, do not lose heart, my friend! Instead I urge you to patiently wait on the Lord who is able to intervene in an extraordinary manner on your behalf. For sure, turning things around in dramatic fashion is one of the hallmarks, one of the trademarks, of God Almighty. Sugar is sweet, gall is bitter, and God is a turn-around God – period!

May 31

Before the mountains were brought forth, or ever thou hadst formed the earth and the world, even from everlasting to everlasting, thou *art* God.

– Psalm 90:2

In March, 2018, a world-renowned scientist was carried to his grave in the U.K. During his lifetime, the eminent scientist invested much of his time and energy in the spread of his atheistic ideas. Now he has passed on. He will certainly not be the last of his kind. Even as I write, several babies who have just arrived on planet earth will grow up one day to challenge the existence of Almighty God. Just sit down to ponder over the matter! The existence of the same Almighty God who offered solace and strength to the likes of Abraham, Moses, Elijah, Elisha; yes the same Almighty God who raised the Lord Jesus Christ from the grave, being challenged by an infant born into the world thousands of years later!

One thing is sure, though; no matter how much energy these ladies and gentlemen of flesh invest to oppose the existence of the Ancient of Days, from Eternity to Eternity His Name shall rule superior.

So let us hold on tenaciously to our faith, my dear Christian friend. Let us not waver, not be discouraged, not give up!

JUNE 1

****
The LORD maketh poor, and maketh rich: he bringeth low, and lifteth up.

– 1 Samuel 2:7

****

Some time ago, I enlisted the services of a PR firm in Cologne, Germany, to help me publicize a German version of one of my books. After getting to know I had just graduated from medical school in his country, he inquired:

"As someone from Africa, your parents must be very rich and influential for you to have been able to study to become a doctor in Europe. How could you otherwise have managed to pay for your education in Germany?"

In reply I made it known to him both of my parents were simple impoverished peasants who struggled from the rising of the tropical sun to its fall to feed themselves and their children.

"How then did you manage to come this far in life?' he wanted to know.

"I was elevated by Mighty Jesus!" was my reply.

"Really?" he inquired, the surprise written on his face

"Yes, for sure. Master Jesus picked me up from the deep dark abyss of poverty I was born into and catapulted me from status nothing to position something!"

Dear Christian soldier, are you being ridiculed by society because of poverty, low birth, barrenness, etc.? I urge you not to lose heart, for surely and certainly Master Jesus who has authority over all that is seen and unseen is capable, in His own time, of promoting you from status nonentity to status entity, from position low to position high, yes indeed, from Mr/Miss/Mrs Naught to Mr/Miss/Mrs Top!!

JUNE 2

****

Rejoice evermore. Pray without ceasing. In everything give thanks: for this is the will of God in Christ Jesus concerning you.

– 1 Thessalonians 5:16-18

****

Accompany us Lord in all that we set out to do today.

May your angels give us a tender touch to awaken us from a deep night's sleep.

As we go to the bathroom to tidy ourselves in preparation for the day's chores, may the heavenly hosts be by our side.

At the breakfast table, we beseech thee to send your spirit to sanctify what by your grace we are privileged to enjoy.

When we leave home for school, work, shopping or to attend to other necessities of life,

may the messengers of heaven still be by our side to drive away any evil from our side.

As we drive our cars through the busy streets may the Heavenly Hosts

still be near us to shield us from sudden misfortune

and help us to be calm and collected even under provocation from other traffic users.

Let our communication with our fellow human beings this day be pure and holy.

Help us to show mercy towards all who may need our help.

Help us also to let our light shine among our fellow human beings that they may see your Kingdom in us and give you the glory.

By a kind word, a loving gesture, a show of kindness, help us to brighten the hearts of others.

Help us also to speak encouraging words to the downhearted and in so doing bring your Kingdom home to their hearts.

When the day's chores outside of the home are over and we head for home, be still our guide and guardian. May our conversation with family members on our return be smooth, loving and uplifting.

When at the long last we retire to our beds, may your divine messengers keep us under their wings that no evil may come near us. We also pray you to dispatch a battalion of angels from Heaven to stand guard around our home to protect us from the terror that strikes at night as well as the pestilence that stalks in the darkness.

In the Name of the Father and the Son and the Holy Spirit, we pray. Amen.

JUNE 3

****

But those who hope in the LORD will renew their strength. They will soar on wings like eagles; they will run and not grow weary, they will walk and not be faint.

– Isaiah 40:31(NIV)

****

I cannot help but admire the long-distance runners of our age when I watch them on TV perform their feat. As I do so, I am inclined to ask myself—how are they able to achieve that! Of course, in such moments we tend to forget the hours of training they had undergone in preparation ahead of the race.

Christians are spiritual marathon runners. We are not sprinters, the likes of Usain Bolt. "P-o-o-o-h!"—there goes the sound of the gun to signify the beginning of the race. Off the sprinters spring from the starting blocks: one, two, three… eight, nine, ten seconds! It is all over; job done! The spectators filling the ninety-thousand seats of the stadium are set in a frenzied ecstasy. They stand in ovation as the successful athlete undertakes a lap of honour!

No, that is not the type of race Christians are engaged in. Our race is more akin to a marathon, run not only on a flat and level field, but also along rough and rugged terrain. Up and down the mountains and hills, along bends and curves, along valleys and plateaus we also run.

At the beginning of the race, the skies may be bright and blue; the good weather may not tarry long, though. Yes, a change of weather may bring strong winds our way, which could soon be followed by rain.

Through all these conditions however we should keep focussed; indeed we must keep our gaze fixed on our goal and patiently run the race set before us so at the end of the day we can claim the victory.

JUNE 4

****
Vanity of vanities, saith the Preacher, vanity of vanities; all is vanity.

– Ecclesiastes 1:2-5

****

It is deceptive, deceptive, the glory of this world.
Today we see them: the powerful politicians of our day;
men and women of power and authority surrounded with pomp and pageantry.
Wherever they go the press, the media, the cameras are there to greet them.
Wherever they step they capture the attention of the public – powerful and majestic they are by the standards of the world.
But lo and behold, they are voted out of office,
and they gradually fade away from the memory of society.
They may be remembered by statues and monuments,
but even such things are not eternal;
an earthquake, a storm or fire, may wipe away such monuments.
There is a Name that will stand for ever, though–the Rock of Ages.
You can invest your hope in Him friend;
you can count on Him, brother;
you can bet on Him, sister.
It is deceptive, deceptive, the glory of this world.

Today we see them – the stars and celebrities of our day, men and women of glamour surrounded with pomp and pageantry.

Wherever they go the media with their set cameras are there to greet them.
Wherever they step they capture the attention
of the public –
powerful and majestic they are by the standards of the world.
But lo and behold, as the years pass by and their beauties and glamour
fade away, they gradually fade away from the
memory of society.
There is a Name that will stand for ever,
a Name that Never fades with time—the Rock of Ages.
That Name will stand forever and ever. AMEN.

JUNE 5

Nevertheless I have somewhat against thee, because thou hast left thy first love. Remember therefore from whence thou art fallen, and repent, and do the first works; or else I will come unto thee quickly, and will remove thy candlestick out of his place, except thou repent.

– Revelation 2:4-6

One day as I was writing on my Laptop, I suddenly heard a peep tone. I wondered what was the matter. Soon the message, the battery is running low, flashed across the screen. I was being asked to take action, yes indeed re-charge my battery, otherwise the device was going to switch off.

That incident led me to pause and reflect. Have I re-charged my spiritual battery not only for that day, but for the several days ahead of me? Dear Christian friend we need indeed to keep our fire burning all the time, a fact which requires that we, on a regular basis, re-charge our battery from the main source of spiritual strength, the Word of God.

The reality is that in the hustle and bustle of today's fast-moving world, it may not always be easy to find the time to do so. It is imperative upon us to strive to do so however, for just in the same way that fire has a tendency to go dim, indeed to become extinguished without input of fuel, in the same way our spiritual flame has a tendency to grow dim, yes even become extinguished without regular input of spiritual fuel.

Let us, dear fellow Christian through regualr prayer and Bible study keep our spiritual torch aglow, so we may be the sources of light in a dark word.

JUNE 6

***

But we preach Christ crucified, unto the Jews a stumbling block, and unto the Greeks foolishness.

– 1 Corinthians 1:23

***

Some, when they get to know I am a doctor, begin to ask: "You are a doctor, and you believe in God?"

I really find the question strange. It is however not unexpected for it is an open secret that many who have passed through the walls of medical schools are among the multitude of humanity who do not believe in the existence of a Creator.

When something goes wrong with my car, I look out for the nearest garage that specialises in my vehicle brand. When I entrust my vehicle to the expert, I do not engage the fellow in conversations as to whether in his opinion the entire vehicle was designed and constructed by someone.

When I open up my computer or laptop to discover the complex manner in which it is built, I do not question how it came to be there. Indeed, I consider it to be a matter of course.

It is only when it comes to the matter of the human body that many, including doctors who have been trained to 'repair' and 'fix' it, begin to reject the fact that indeed someone was responsible for designing it, indeed creating it!

How can anyone shut his or her eyes to the fact that there is indeed an Intelligence Designer, a Creator God behind the human body—the body made up among others of multi-complex organs such as the brain, the heart, the liver, etc.?

My dear Christian soldier, please join me in prayer today for those blind to things of the spiritual realm, yes for those who are still struggling to come to grips with what can only be discerned with the eye of faith.

June 7

> But the natural man receiveth not the things of the Spirit of God: for they are foolishness unto him: neither can he know them, because they are spiritually discerned.
>
> – 1 Corinthians 2:14

When we are touched by the Good shepherd and we are able, by His grace, to discern spiritual things, we are elevated to a different plane of human existence. In such a situation, we are privileged for example to understand that natural impossibilities cannot obstruct the working of the Holy One. We have no problem in believing that the Lord can walk on water, raise the dead, yes even resurrect the dead.

Some may probably call us stupid or naive, for believing what they may describe as fairy tales—but that is their problem, not ours. We do not wish to use derogating terms like stupid to describe them. We are free, however, with no offence intended, to describe them as blind, not physically, but spiritually. We cannot on our own heal their spiritual blindness. We can however pray for them; yes, in prayer we should bring them before Almighty God and plead with Him to heal them of their spiritual blindness.

Freely we have received, freely they can also be given. They have to humble themselves, though; it may otherwise happen that by virtue of being self-conceited, they miss the opportunity to jump on the salvation train.

Let's not be weary of spreading the Hope of Salvation to a lost world, my dear Christian friends.

JUNE 8

****

And Elisha prayed, and said, LORD, I pray thee, open his eyes, that he may see. And the LORD opened the eyes of the young man; and he saw: and, behold, the mountain *was* full of horses and chariots of fire round about Elisha.

– 2 Kings 6:17

****

"Lord, I pray thee open his eyes, that he may see."

Before I made a decision to follow the Lord, I did not count myself among the atheists. I did believe in the existence of God. Still, the problems of the world was making me, if not to question His existence, to struggle to commit myself to Him.

Then came my own born-again experience, an experience "which opened my eyes" so I could see beyond the physical world.

I must say that I have experienced even more personal suffering, set-backs, more emotional anguish, distressing situations, etc., after my conversion, than prior to my conversion.

Yet the difficulties and challenges have not caused me to abandon my faith. Why not? The reason is not far-fetched: by His grace, I am now able to see beyond the now, beyond the personal challenges, the disasters, the earthquakes, the terror attacks, the heinous crimes, indeed beyond the darkness of the present time to behold the glory to come.

Our duty, fellow Christians, is not only to spread the news of salvation to the unbeliever. Like the Prophet Elisha we also have a duty to pray the Lord to open the eyes of those we witness to, that "they may see", indeed, see beyond the mere physical world to behold the spiritual realm of our existence .

JUNE 9

****
And it came to pass after these things, that God did prove Abraham, and said unto him, Abraham; and he said, Here am I. And he said, Take now thy son, thine only son, whom thou lovest, even Isaac, and get thee into the land of Moriah; and offer him there for a burnt offering upon one of the mountains which I will tell thee of.

– Genesis 22:1-2
****

Abraham, Abraham, Abraham! I am not speaking for him, but I can imagine Abraham saying at some point in his walk with the Lord:

"Mighty God, why didn't you choose someone else!! Yes, if I had really known how things were going to work out, I would have stayed back in my little town *Ur of the Chaldeans.*"

The reader may be familiar with the strings of trials the "poor soul" Abraham had to go through:

Almighty God commanded him to leave his native land. He tried him, suffering him to wander as a stranger in the land given him by promise. He tried him in the peril of Sarah in Egypt and in the peril of Lot in Sodom. He tried him in causing him to wait twenty-five long years before Isaac was born. He tried him severely when He bade him thrust out his son Ishmael from his home...

One might have thought, that was surely the end of all his tests, his exams, if you like.

But no! Almighty God demanded from Professor Abraham, Doctor of Trials and Affliction, yet another, more challenging test, with a much greater degree of difficulty! Just as he probably thought he had done his very best and had sat for his last degree in the University of Trials and Afflictions, he was called upon to sit for yet another paper to prove his worth!

"No, please! I don't want to be dubbed the Perpetual Student of Humanity. Please look for someone else, my nephew Lot, for example." Thus Abraham might have protested! But no, he had to endure yet another trial—the most challenging of all.

Dear Christian soldier, do you have the impression you have also become a perpetual student of affliction—one affliction ending only for the next challenge to begin. Do not lose heart, fellow soldier. Do not lose heart. The future will not be in perpetual darkness; surely, the sun will rise to signal the beginning of a new day in your life.

JUNE 10

****
Be strong and of a good courage, fear not, nor be afraid of them: for the Lord thy God, he it is that doth go with thee; he will not fail thee, nor forsake thee.

– Deuteronomy 31:6
****

The 14th of September, 2018, heralded the 40th anniversary of my decision to follow the Lord. I won't be telling the truth if I were to declare here that my Christian journey has been a bed of roses all along. I have indeed over the period experienced my ups and downs. I would be on the mountain of joy at one moment only to stumble in my valley of despair and despondency moments later.

On not a few occasions, it felt to me as if there was no way out of my problems. I turned to the right and to the left, I looked up and then down, I stepped backwards and then forwards—no help seemed to be forthcoming. Stuck in the seemingly hopeless situation, I did not envisage, at least from the human point of view, how things could take a different turn.

Almighty God who knows the heart of men bears me witness that on some occasions I was so overwhelmed by my situation, I was tempted to heed the advice of Job's wife and "curse God and die". Then said his wife unto him, Dost thou still retain thine integrity? curse God, and die (Job 2:9-10).

Today, looking back to those despairing moments of my Christian walk, I am indeed ashamed at myself for having been led to question the love of He who was faithful yesterday, and who is faithful today and who shall evermore remain faithful to those who call on Him.

Friend, I do not know the problems confronting you; neither am I aware of your prayer request(s) to the Lord. One thing I can assure you is that He in whom you have placed your trust is faithful and will not allow you to be tempted beyond what you are capable of bearing!

June 11

****

Assemble yourselves and come; draw near together, ye that are escaped of the nations: they have no knowledge that set up the wood of their graven image, and pray unto a god that cannot save.

– Isaiah 45:20

****

Today's verse brings to my mind the text of a Ghanaian gospel song I was listening to the other day. The singer, who happened to be a pastor, said in his song that he was aware of individuals who carry their gods with them, in the form of rings on their fingers. He went on to state that should such individuals happen to be away from home and all of a sudden come to the realization they had forgotten their protecting ring(s) at home, they are scared to death for fear something sinister might befall them! Deprived of their presumed source of protection, such individuals begin to panic and fear the worst.

In the little village in Ghana where my late mother was born, a form of traditional African worship is practiced. It is customary for adherents of that religion, at the beginning of each year, to pledge a lump sum of money to the gods to solicit their protection from evil in the course of that particular year. Why pledge allegiance to ordinary idols rather than to He who controls the oxygen ventilating our lungs!

Fellow Christian soldiers, let us be assured that as long as we stay true to our calling, no weapons formed against us shall proper. So let us not be fearful of the forces up in arms against us. Let us rather keep marching on and keep pushing forward with all boldness towards the New Jerusalem.

June 12

***

And Elisha prayed, and said, LORD, I pray thee, open his eyes, that he may see. And the LORD opened the eyes of the young man; and he saw: and, behold, the mountain *was* full of horses and chariots of fire round about Elisha

– 2 Kings 6:17

***

When I was in medical school one of our anatomy professors, his head bubbling with much knowledge of his sphere of study, lectured with all enthusiasm about how through the process of evolution, the various organs of the human body adapted themselves to assume the functions they are capable of performing now!!

As I sat listening to him, I prayed to El Shaddai, God Almighty, to heal him of his spiritual blindness, to comprehend things of the Divine. Just as in the case of Elisha's servant, many are going about afflicted with spiritual blindness. Unable to discern things of the spiritual realm, they limit themselves to the physical, they use their physical senses to interpret things from the material point of view. Blinded in matters relating to the spiritual realm, they go about spreading the false notion that chance has created the universe including themselves.

Dear Christian friends, please join me in prayer for the lost; yes, that they, like Elisha's servant, will have their eyes opened that they may see!

June 13

****

Be careful for nothing; but in everything by prayer and supplication with thanksgiving let your requests be made known unto God.

– Philippians 4:6

****

We are called upon to bring our prayer requests to the Lord and trust him to sort things out for us. That does not imply, however, that we should sit idly by and not undertake what is within our means to do to solve the problems that come our way. For instance, if we are unemployed, we should not hope for employment without applying for jobs and attending interviews if we are called to do so. As we put our best foot forward, we are called upon to pray for guidance and trust Him for an outcome that is in line with His will.

Cultivating a sense of dependence on Him will keep us calm and stable no matter the circumstances. Our circumstances, like the weather, may change at short notice. Well, in this regard, readers who live in a place like Ghana which enjoys a fairly stable weather regime may not grasp what I'm driving at. On the other hand, those resident in a place like the UK where the weather has the tendency to change at short notice, surely will. In the same way that the weather in the British Isles can turn from good to bad at short notice, our joyful circumstances may become sorrowful tomorrow.

Let us pray the Lord to help us bring our troubles and challenges to him in prayer, rather than keep them on our minds and be tormented by sleepless nights.

JUNE 14

****
Go to now, ye that say, Today or tomorrow we will go into such a city, and continue there a year, and buy and sell, and get gain: Whereas ye know not what shall be on the morrow. For what is your life? It is even a vapour, that appeareth for a little time, and then vanisheth away. For that ye ought to say, If the Lord will, we shall live, and do this, or that.

– James 4:13-15
****

On Tuesday February 26, 2008, I retired to bed as usual around 10:30pm. I went to bed with high hopes as well as plans and ideas for the future.

Then it all happened...

As if in a dream, I heard the rumbling and violent shaking of the whole house. It sounded just like a jumbo jet, after a long flight, touches down on the tarmac and decelerates along the runway to a halt.

'That was an earthquake!' began Rita my wife.

Just then the cry of "Mama! Mama! What is going on?" emanated from the room of Jonathan, the youngest of our three children.

Moments later he ran into our room. Out of fear he refused to return to his room for the rest of the night.

Yes indeed, an earthquake had struck...

I took a look at the clock. It was exactly 01:00 hrs GMT Wednesday the 27th of February 2008.

In the course of the morning further details emerged in regard to the earthquake.

It was said to be the strongest of its kind to have hit the UK for nearly 25 years and shook homes across large parts of England.

Over the next several days I reflected on the matter. In the event, the fact that I am in transit on planet earth, and that the connecting flight, DEATH AIRLINES, might arrive at any time to take me to my final destination, came home to me even more powerfully than before.

Whereas it is legitimate for us to make plans for tomorrow, we should, fellow Christian soldiers, always be conscious of the fact that the future is not our own, but belongs to the Lord.

June 15

****
For we wrestle not against flesh and blood, but against principalities, against powers, against the rulers of the darkness of this world, against spiritual wickedness in high places.

– Ephesians 6:12
****

When I got to Year 5 at primary school, I was afflicted by an ailment to my left ankle. Unable to weight-bear on the affected leg, it led me to stay away from school for two years.

Apart from taking me to hospital , my parents also consulted traditional healers in their desperate attempt to help their little son. Some of the methods applied by the traditional healers could be described as horrific, to put it mildly. Probably to ensure a more intense penetration of the mixture into the body, some pf them first inflicted several cuts on the skin of the affected joint before applying their medicine, usually in the form of a cream. Since some of the ingredients included ginger, one can imagine the burning sensation I had to endure!

In another instance, the healer we consulted prepared a concoction of herbs that he brought to the boil in a large black pot on an open fire. Next, he took hold of a small razor blade and inflicted several cuts to the skin over the sick joint. Then he called for four young men in the neighbourhood to hold me firmly down. Finally, he grasped the afflicted left leg firmly and brought it in position close to the mouth of the boiling pot! The steam coming from the boiling mixture, he explained, did not only carry healing powers but was capable of neutralising the spell cast on my leg by evil forces. I screamed at the top of my voice as the steam burnt my skin.

"You have to bear it, my little boy; that is the only way I can help you!" he consoled me. Big drops of sweat covered my body as I screamed at the top of my voice. That did not deter him as he continued to hold on firmly to my ailing leg. Finally, after keeping me in that position for several minutes, he asked the young men to carry me back to my seat.

My dear Christian friend, do you have the impressions you are being tormented by the Devil, yes by the forces up against you?

In my case, my 'tormentors' meant it for my good; certainly, none of them harboured malicious intentions. They wanted to see me healed of my ailment—only the means to that end caused me severe pain.

Let us not be scared by the antics of Satan and his host of principalities, though. They will come to nought, for we have Almighty God for protection!

June 16

****

Go to the ant, thou sluggard; consider her ways, and be wise.

– Proverbs 6:6

****

As I was growing up in my little village, there was an elderly distant relative who was admired by all for being very hard-working. Whereas everyone in the little community went about their daily activities with zeal, he played in a different league when it came to our fellow resident, Papa Kwabena.

It was his custom to leave the village early in the morning to work on his farm. In the afternoon, one might see him returning from the fields with a heavy load made up of all possible items on his head as well as on both shoulders. One would be mistaken, then, to presume that his daily chores had ended! No! After he had rested for a while, he got up once more, took his machete and headed for the woods yet again! One could only wonder what was driving him to the woods at that time of day. Was he on his way to inspect the traps he had set for rodents such as the grass cutter? Was he on his way to the Nwi River to inspect his fish traps? Was he on his way to get some assignment done on another field?

Two or three hours later one would find him returning to the village, once again bearing a heavy load. Even then it would be premature to conclude that the daily chores of this extraordinarily diligent resident were over for the day. No! Minutes later he would be seen heading for the woods for the third time—only God knew what for!

Whilst we are not called upon to be extremely industrious, indeed to the point of over-exerting ourselves, it is nevertheless true that we need to make a decent effort to cater for ourselves as well as for those who depend on us.

Indeed, while "all hard work brings a profit," it's also true that "mere talk leads only to poverty." Proverbs 14:23(NIV)

JUNE 17

****
There was a man of the Pharisees, named Nicodemus, a ruler of the Jews: The same came to Jesus by night, and said unto him, Rabbi, we know that thou art a teacher come from God: for no man can do these miracles that thou doest, except God be with him.

– John 3:1- 2
****

"The same came to Jesus by night."

The question worthy of asking is—why did he come by night and not by day?

The respected Professor that He was, he was nevertheless ashamed to be seen visiting Jesus by day. It is strange but true that the more one becomes educated in matters of this world, the more one is inclined to disbelief in God or, as in the case of Nicodemus, to confess Him openly.

Education of course is good; wisdom of course is good. The question that arises is: what is education all about? Is it not acquiring knowledge about things related to the universe—the universe created by Almighty God?!

Certainly, over the years Mankind has acquired great knowledge in several areas related to the universe. Such knowledge has been applied in various ways and has led to several inventions.

I shall cite here the example of the invention of the jet engine—what a great feat of engineering! But what is all the fuss about our modern inventions? Indeed, we must learn to put everything in perspective. For example, does the fact that Mankind has been able to devise an engine capable of generating a powerful pushing force or thrust capable of lifting a plane of monstrous size and weight into the air mean we are also capable of defeating the ageing process, indeed of conquer death?

Does the fact that we have, for example, been able to decipher the DNA imply we should not honour He who created all things in the first place—including the DNA?

WE should indeed, learn to assign honour where honour is due, for at the end of the day the knowledge acquired by even the most adored scientist, yes, the so-called 'super brains', the Einsteins of our age, amount to only a tiny, indeed a microscopic fraction of the vast expanse of God's Creation.

So dear Christian soldiers, let us not be intimidated into keeping silent by the so-called Professors and experts of our times. They are accounted for nothing, before our Great High God.

JUNE 18

****

Jesus said to him, "Thomas, because you have seen Me, you have believed. Blessed *are* **those who have not seen and** *yet* **have believed."**

– John 20:29

****

This Bible passage may be familiar to many of us. In our day, there are those who seem to create the impression of only wanting to believe in God when they see Him! Why adopt such an attitude?

Do we switch on our radio every morning because we see the radio waves with our naked eye, or do we do so because we believe they exist?

When we dial numbers on our mobile phone in expectation of speaking to our dear ones, do we do so because we see the waves with our own eyes?

Those who, like Thomas, resort to adopting the "seeing is believing" excuse only need to cast their glance at the world around them, to behold the Hand of God at work in the Universes.

God's creation is indeed huge. The birds of the air, the lilies of the field, the vast oceans, the huge mountains, etc., all point to the Hand of an Intelligent Designer, Almighty God, in the universe.

Dear Christian soldiers, let us remember the doubting Thomases of this world in prayer that they might come to know the truth, and that the truth will set them free.

June 19

****

Therefore all things whatsoever ye would that men should do to you, do ye even so to them: for this is the law and the prophets.

– Matthew 7:12

****

Once a patient of mine spoke about the agony she went through when she found out her very best friend was having an affair with her husband. It would have been painful if he had gone with a stranger, but when it involves your own best friend it is even more agonizing.

Surely, dear reader, you might also have heard something similar.

'And the second *is* like, *namely* this, Thou shalt love thy neighbour as thyself. There is no other commandment greater than these. Mark 12:31

Of course, I do believe the Lord Jesus is the son of God. Even if we put that fact aside and followed only His teachings, how much misery would be avoided in this our wicked world!

On the human-to-human level, vices like envy, jealousy, back biting, racism, gang culture, tribalism, feuds, etc., would be a thing of the past.

On the corporate level, there will be more healthy competition among business partners; on a nation-to-nation basis, relations will be pursued on a more just and fairer basis.

Of course, my dear Christian friend, we have not got to the New Jerusalem yet—we are still in the wilderness. Indeed, we are left with nothing other than prayer, praying for the Holy Spirit to give us the needed grace to enable us to do the very little we can to let our light shine wherever we are.

June 20

But they that wait upon the Lord shall renew their strength; they shall mount up with wings as eagles; they shall run, and not be weary; and they shall walk, and not faint.

– Isaiah 40:31

Let us wait on the Lord labourers of the Cross,
Let us be patient in waiting;
And never allow the circumstances to overwhelm us as we wait on our faithful Friend.
The delay may be long and distressing;
still, let us not to grow weary
for we are waiting on no other than the Lord Jesus!

Let us wait on the Lord, servants of the cross,
Let us not lose heart waiting!
He has been tried and proven faithful under all circumstances!
Come what may, He surely will visit our home to turn our situation around.
So let us not grow weary in waiting, for He in whom we have placed our trust is faithful and will not allow us to be tempted beyond our ability to cope. Surely in his own right time He will shine on our homes to turn our nights into day!

June 21

****

Then the king commanded, and they brought Daniel, and cast him into the den of lions. Now the king spake and said unto Daniel, Thy God whom thou servest continually, he will deliver thee.

– Daniel 6:16

****

Do you have the impression that the principalities up against you are threatening to seize you and throw you into a spiritual 'lions' den', to be devoured by the hungry lions being kept there? Do not be frightened by their threats, dear Christian soldier.

You may as well urge the Enemy to gather not only a few, but rather a multitude of fearful-looking lions and keep them in wait for you. You may as well urge your foes, yes those devolving malicious schemes against you, to go a step further and add a host of tigers, wolves, crocodiles, bears, hyenas, pythons to the fierce-looking lions already eagerly waiting for you. Even in that threatening situation, you need not fear. Instead, keep on waving the Christian banner and do not allow yourself to be intimidated.

Yes indeed, child of God, do not be scared; even though the witches, wizards, principalities—you can go on naming them—in high and low places, from the four corners of the earth, join forces against you, they will never succeed in harming you, indeed, in bringing their schemes to bear on you!

So fellow Christian, let's keep marching fearlessly on, towards the New Jerusalem!

JUNE 22

****
When you go through deep waters, I will be with you.
— Isaiah 43:2
****

That is comforting and soothing at the same time—to be assured of Divine presence in time of need!

Every Christian from time to time may have to go through 'deep waters'. It is part of our human existence on a fallen planet.

Child or God, are you going through your deep waters? Are the waters rising, rising and rising—first knee level, then up to the navel, then the nipples. I see your lower jaw is now submerged in the still rising waters!

You are looking round for help—but help seems nowhere near! The situation is desperate; the outlook is grim, really grim. You turn your gaze to the heavens, and things don't look promising for the skies are not clear and bright. Instead of a bright blue sky, you behold the gathering clouds announcing the imminent onset of yet more rains!

Even in such a harrowing state of affairs, do not lose hope for He who promised to be with you in deep waters is faithful and will keep his word; he will not abandon you, nor leave you to the mercy of the elements.

So, cheer up, despairing child of God, and await your sure rescue!

JUNE 23

****

Why art thou cast down, O my soul? and why art thou disquieted within me? hope thou in God: for I shall yet praise him, who is the health of my countenance, and my God.

– Psalm 42:11

****

Friend, you may today be bearing a cross, a cross that is so heavy it threatens to break your neck. Pray to heaven for the grace to bear it, pray to heaven for the strength to persevere; pray to the Divine to bestow upon you the strength and grace to endure as you await the mysterious hand of the Loving One to bring a change in your situation—to turn your cross into a crown of glory.

Oh, I can see Heaven has already dispatched angels to your assistance! So, stand up and begin to dance, child of God! Shake, shake your body; brush off the dust of depression, of resignation, of the negative thoughts that beset you, which cause you to be cast down by a feeling of helplessness and sadness!

Tell the feeling of gloom to leave your home, the atmosphere of dejection to leave your living room, the spirit of negative thoughts to take flight and flee. "Hey you, Negative thoughts, you spirit of depression clouding the thoughts of my fellow Christian soldier, I charge you in the Almighty Name of the Lord to flee. Flee, flee, in Jesus' name!"

JUNE 24

****
"I can do all things through Christ who strengthens me."
– Philippians 4:13
****

With the Lord on his or her side, the Christian soldier need not fear what tomorrow will bring. Wealth cannot give us that assurance, for as the saying goes, money has a way of taking wings and flying.

We might have heard or read about instances when millionaires have gone bankrupt, indeed have lost all or almost all.

A crash of the Global financial market, the likes of what was witnessed in 1998 could lead to the wiping away of our investments.

Our properties, yes real estate investment, cannot offer perfect security—the earth on which they are built can quake to send them crumbling.

Political heavyweights, those who wield authority, the likes of the President of the US, when they leave office become ordinary citizens.

Christian soldier, let us build on the Lord! Yes, let us draw close to Him, for indeed, it is He alone who can see us through our problems, however mighty they might be.

JUNE 25

****

The Lord will cause your enemies who rise against you to be defeated before you. They shall come out against you one way and flee before you seven ways.

– Deuteronomy 28:7

****

When I was in Year 8 in school, I accompanied some of my mates to empty the letterbox of our school. It was a time of youthful exuberance, adventure and banter! After we had collected our mail, someone suggested we tried our key in other letterboxes. One of them, probably without an owner, happened to be unlocked. The moment one of my mates inserted the key into it, it opened! Just at that very moment the postmaster, a very stern person in his forties, appeared from nowhere! He accused us of attempted theft. For reasons best known to himself, he singled me out for blame. He wouldn't let the matter rest. He held me by the collar of my shirt and dragged me to the local police station, a stone's throw away. Was it because the police did not want to incur the displeasure of one of the influential residents of the settlement? I cannot tell for sure, but one thing happened for sure—they decided to lock me up in one of their cells! The news of my detention spread like wildfire.

Eventually, after spending several hours behind bars, my father managed to convince them to set me free!

Dear Christina friend, do you have the impression that the devil has picked you out, yes, singled you out of the crowd for special attention?

Indeed, whereas your peers, your schoolmates, your social media friends, yes everyone seems to be progressing, you are struggling to make ends meet. You are not by any means lazy! Indeed, you have made your very best effort—to no avail. To make things even worse, you have recently been a victim of online scam, wiping away the very last savings you can boast of! I have a word for you, dear Child of God: do not fear, for "the *Lord will cause your enemies who rise against you to be defeated before you. They shall come out against you one way and flee before you seven ways.*"

JUNE 26

****

Come unto me, all ye that labour and are heavy laden, and I will give you rest. Take my yoke upon you, and learn of me; for I am meek and lowly in heart: and ye shall find rest unto your souls. For my yoke is easy, and my burden is light.

– Matthew 11:28-30

****

Burdens we all carry. Indeed, the list of burdens afflicting mankind is endless.

Society seem to think that those who are successful in their respective spheres of activity, have no burdens to bear. Indeed, we seem to fancy that if we became millionaires or even billionaires our burdens will go away. Not on our fallen planet, dear friend, not on our fallen planet! Becoming a millionaire could, perhaps, eliminate our material burdens; not so our spiritual loads.

Some of us were abused as children; yes, we could have been sexually abused as children. The recollection of our painful past coupled with the present difficulties may result in depression, mental agony, a sense of hopelessness, etc.

Some of us are afflicted with the burden of a troubled relationship. Much as we do our best to bring harmony to our home, discord seems to hold permanent sway over our affairs.

"Come unto me all ye that labour and are heavy laden, and I will give you rest." The logical inference from this Divine call is to see the whole of mankind lining up before the Lord, one after the other, to lay before Him their respective burdens, yes the burdens plaguing them and threatening to break their necks.

The reality though is that for whatever reason, many of us prefer to bear our burdens alone.

Dear Christian friends, let us learn to bring our burdens, however many, yes however heavy, before the Great Burden bearer instead of seeking to carry them on our own.

June 27

****
But my God shall supply all your need according to his riches in glory by Christ Jesus.

– **Philippians 4:19**
****

Are you hard pressed financially? One misfortune after the other has perhaps set in to adversely affect your business; your business balance sheet is not good; worse still—your bills are piling up.

Your corporation tax is in arrears, your utility bills are piling up, your children's school fees are due. Several direct debits have been returned; more are due to be returned.

Your bank has written to warn you concerning the outstanding mortgage payment. You have a last chance to meet your commitments or face eviction—you have been warned.

Winter is setting in, the bitter winters of the northern hemisphere—forecasters are predicting an extremely severe winter. You just read in the newspapers the case of someone who was evicted into the bitter cold of winter. The thought that it could soon be your turn has sent cold shivers down your spine.

Dear Christian soldier, even in your obviously dreadful situation, I urge you to keep on hoping and trusting in the Lord.

JUNE 28

****
These things I have spoken unto you, that in me ye might have peace. In the world ye shall have tribulation: but be of good cheer; I have overcome the world.

– John 16:33
****

Reflecting on the above verse, E.G. White, one of the founders of the SDA church, wrote: "Christ did not fail, neither was He discouraged, and His followers are to manifest a faith of the same enduring nature. They are to live as He lived, and work as He worked, because they depend on Him as the great Master Worker. Courage, energy, and perseverance they must possess. Though apparent impossibilities obstruct their way, by His grace they are to go forward. Instead of deploring difficulties, they are called upon to surmount them. They are to despair of nothing, and to hope for everything."

With the above words of encouragement, I wish you a blessed day, fellow soldier of Christ.

June 29

****

Ye are the light of the world. A city that is set on an hill cannot be hid. Neither do men light a candle, and put it under a bushel, but on a candlestick; and it giveth light unto all that are in the house. Let your light so shine before men, that they may see your good works, and glorify your Father which is in heaven.

— Matthew 5:14-16

****

When I was growing up in my little village, there was no electricity.

It turned dark, very dark, around 6:30pm and remained dark till around 6am the next morning.

The only source of light for our whole household were two Swiss kerosene lamps. We, the "junior academics" of the home, assembled around one of them to get our homework done. The rest of the family made use of the remaining one to go about their activities.

The bleak outlook in the nights was interrupted for a period of about ten days every month with the appearance of the moon in the nightly skies.

The appearance of the moon livened the nightly life activities of the village. Residents, especially the children and teenagers, took advantage of the 'natural electricity' as we termed the bright moonlight nights, and engaged in various kinds of games.

Dear Christian friends, Our Master calls us the light of the world. We are indeed the only source of radiance in a very dark world.

It is therefore imperative on our part to let our light shine wherever we are to illuminate the surrounding darkness. To be able to keep on shining, we on our part have constantly to draw from the source of light, otherwise we are in danger of turning dim, yes going off, and submerging the world into even deeper darkness.

JUNE 30

And Gideon said unto him, Oh my Lord, if the LORD be with us, why then is all this befallen us? and where be all his miracles which our fathers told us of, saying, Did not the LORD bring us up from Egypt? but now the LORD hath forsaken us, and delivered us into the hands of the Midianites.

– Judges 6:13

It cannot be, it cannot be! If there is a God who cares, if all that the Bible says is true, why then is He not coming to my rescue?

If there is a Lord who cares, if all that is written in His word is true, why then has He allowed all this misery to visit my home?

If there is a Lord who cares, if all that the Bible proclaims about Him is true, why then did He not prevent the death of my dear spouse?

If there is a Lord who cares, if all that the Bible declares concerning Him is true, why then did He not prevent the breakdown of my business?

Since I made a decision to follow Him, I have gone to great lengths to live in accordance with His word. I have been a regular attendant at church, a generous giver not only to His cause but also to alleviate the suffering of others in accordance with the teachings of the Bible. Why then should Almighty God permit such misfortune to visit my home!

Thus the evil one speaks to the hearts of the multitudes of fellow Christian soldiers battling with trials of all sorts!

Let us be brave and courageous, fellow Christian soldier, and not give our ears to the insinuations of the Evil One! Let us instead pray to the Lord for the grace to endure the afflictions that may come our way.

Stay blessed my dear Christian friend.

www.ingramcontent.com/pod-product-compliance
Lightning Source LLC
LaVergne TN
LVHW051547070426
835507LV00021B/2455